Perceptions of Teaching and l

BERA Dialogues

Other Books in the Series

Emerging Partnerships: Current Research in Language and Literacy
  DAVID WRAY (ed.)
Local Management of Schools
  GWEN WALLACE (ed.)
The Management of Change
  PAMELA LOMAX (ed.)
Managing Better Schools and Colleges
  PAMELA LOMAX (ed.)
Managing Staff Development in Schools
  PAMELA LOMAX (ed.)
Performance Indicators
  C. T. FITZ-GIBBON (ed.)
Policy Issues in National Assessment
  P. BROADFOOT *et al.* (eds)

Other Books of Interest

Critical Theory and Classroom Talk
  ROBERT YOUNG
Education of Chinese Children in Britain and the USA
  LORNITA YUEN-FAN WONG
Equality Matters
  H. CLAIRE, J. MAYBIN and J. SWANN (eds)
Language, Minority Education and Gender
  DAVID CORSON
One Europe - 100 Nations
  ROY N. PEDERSEN
Psychology, Spelling and Education
  C. STERLING and C. ROBSON (eds)
School to Work in Transition in Japan
  KAORI OKANO
Sustaining Local Literacies
  DAVID BARTON (ed.)
Teaching-and-Learning Language-and-Culture
  MICHAEL BYRAM, CAROL MORGAN and colleagues

Please contact us for the latest book information:
**Multilingual Matters Ltd, Frankfurt Lodge, Clevedon Hall,
Victoria Road, Clevedon, Avon BS21 7SJ, England**

BERA Dialogues 8
Series Editor: Donald McIntyre

Perceptions of Teaching and Learning

Edited by
Martin Hughes

MULTILINGUAL MATTERS LTD
Clevedon • Philadelphia • Adelaide

Library of Congress Cataloging in Publication Data

Perceptions of Teaching and Learning/Edited by Martin Hughes
p. cm. (BERA Dialogues: 8)
Includes bibliographical references and index.
1. Teachers–Great Britain–Attitudes. 2. Students–Great Britain–Attitudes.
3. Language arts–Great Britain. 4. Educational tests and measurements–
Great Britain. 5. Curriculum change–Great Britain. 6. Educational
surveys–Great Britain.
I. Hughes, Martin. II. Series.
LB1775.4.G7P47   1994
371.1'00941–dc20   93-50123

British Library Cataloguing in Publication Data

A CIP catalogue record for this book is available from the British Library.

ISBN 1-85359-231-5 (pbk)

Multilingual Matters Ltd

UK: Frankfurt Lodge, Clevedon Hall, Victoria Road, Clevedon, Avon BS21 7SJ.
USA: 1900 Frost Road, Suite 101, Bristol, PA 19007, USA.
Australia: P.O. Box 6025, 83 Gilles Street, Adelaide, SA 5000, Australia.

Printed and bound in Great Britain by WBC Ltd, Bridgend.

Contents

List of Contributors

Christopher Brumfit: *School of Education, University of Southampton*
Paul Cooper: *Department of Educational Studies, University of Oxford*
Charles Desforges: *School of Education, University of Exeter*
Susan Harris: *Division of Education, University of Sheffield*
Cathie Holden: *School of Education, University of Exeter*
Janet Hooper: *School of Education, University of Southampton*
Martin Hughes: *School of Education, University of Exeter*
Donald McIntyre: *Department of Educational Studies, University of Oxford*
Rosamond Mitchell: *School of Education, University of Southampton*
Penny Munn: *Department of Psychology, University of Strthclyde*
Ian Plewis: *Thomas Coram Research Unit, University of London*
Jean Rudduck: *Division of Education, University of Sheffield*
Marijcke Veltman: *Thomas Coram Research Unit, University of London*

Introduction

MARTIN HUGHES

This book is about the perceptions of teaching and learning which are held by those who are most closely involved in the educational process or affected by it — such as teachers, pupils and parents. The perceptions described here range from those of nursery staff working with children before they start school, to those of pupils and teachers in the early stages of secondary school. The issues covered include the nature of pre-school learning, the changing primary curriculum, the value of assessment, the seriousness of learning, the role of knowledge about language, and the nature of effective teaching and learning. Taken together, these perceptions provide some important insights into what is currently happening in our education system.

The book is one of the first products to emerge from a research programme funded by the Economic and Social Research Council (ESRC) and entitled 'Innovation and Change in Education: The Quality of Teaching and Learning'. The overall aim of the programme is to increase our understanding of the quality of teaching and learning in a variety of curricula settings and in the context of radical changes in educational policy. In order to meet this aim, ten projects have been funded over the period 1991–95 at a number of centres in England and Scotland. Six of the ten projects presented their initial findings in a symposium at the 1992 BERA Conference in Stirling, and the chapters in this book are based directly on the papers presented at that symposium.

The chapters follow the order of presentation of the papers at the symposium. They fall into two main groups, according to the age of pupils involved.

The first chapter, by Penny Munn, deals with teaching and learning in the preschool, and how this is perceived by staff in preschool centres. Munn describes how the traditional preschool curriculum is under 'downward pressure' from the changes currently underway in the primary curriculum, and sets out to describe how staff are responding to this pressure. Drawing on data from individual interviews and group discussions, she argues that the way in which nursery staff talk about teaching and learning is strongly influenced by the institutional setting in which they work, and in particular by the presence or absence of a teacher in guiding the curriculum. One of the main implications of Munn's research is that we must take full account of the patterns of discourse to be found in an institution if we want to understand the perceptions of those who work in that institution.

The second chapter, by Ian Plewis and Marijcke Veltman, is concerned with changes to the curriculum at Key Stage One (5–7 years). The study on which this chapter is based is unusual, in that it aims to make direct comparisons between what is currently happening in infant classrooms and data collected in the same schools in the early 1980s. In their chapter, Plewis and Veltman discuss some of the methodological problems in making such comparisons. One important distinction they make is between the planned curriculum — the one represented in official documents and guidelines; the enacted curriculum — the one implemented by teachers in the classroom; and the experienced curriculum — the one actually received by the pupils. Plewis and Veltman thus draw our attention to the fact that there are (at least) three separate and potentially different perceptions of what is supposedly the same curriculum — the perceptions of planners, of teachers, and of pupils.

The chapter by Charles Desforges, Martin Hughes and Cathie Holden is also concerned with Key Stage One. Here the focus is on the standardised assessment procedures (SATs) which were first introduced for 7-year-olds in the summer of 1991. The authors compare and contrast the perceptions of two groups who were closely involved in the assessment process — teachers and parents. Their initial findings suggests some important differences between these two groups: while the parents expected the assessments would generate useful information, the teachers did not. Moreover, the teachers seemed mostly unaware of what their parents actually thought about these issues. As Desforges, Hughes and Holden point out, this finding has important implications for the new 'market' ethos in education: schools cannot provide 'what the customers want' if they are unaware of their customers' views.

The remaining three chapters in the book are concerned with children at Key Stage Three (11–14 years). The first of these, by Susan Harris and Jean Rudduck, draws on data collected during the first year of a longitudinal study which is following a group of pupils through four years at three contrasting schools. The chapter uses material from a number of sources, including interviews with pupils and teachers, to examine the strategies used by schools to signal the importance of learning in Years 7 and 8, and the way these are perceived by the pupils themselves. Two key concepts used by Harris and Rudduck are 'membership' and 'labelling', which, they argue, have a strong influence on pupils' attitudes towards the seriousness of learning. One conclusion drawn by Harris and Rudduck is that the excitements and upheavals of the first few terms in secondary school can easily overshadow the new demands of academic learning, and that teachers may be unaware of the extent to which this is so.

The chapter by Rosamond Mitchell, Christopher Brumfit and Janet Hooper focuses on the place of 'knowledge about language' in English and foreign language teaching. The authors review the recent history of this contentious issue, and argue that the debate has taken place with very little empirical knowledge of how language is viewed by teachers and pupils, how it is actually talked about in language classrooms, and what kinds of models and understandings are developed by pupils. The study described by Mitchell, Brumfit and Hooper aims to provide such data by observing and recording in Year 9 classrooms, by interviewing pupils and teachers, and by designing specific activities focusing on different aspects of knowledge about language. One initial finding emerging from the study is that there are substantial differences between English and foreign language classrooms in the way that 'knowledge about language' is dealt with: this finding may have considerable implications for pupils' attempts to integrate their learning experiences across subject boundaries.

The last chapter in the book, by Paul Cooper and Donald McIntyre, is concerned with pupils' and teachers' perceptions of effective teaching and learning in the classroom. The chapter draws on observations made in English and history lessons involving Year 7 pupils, and on subsequent interviews with both pupils and teachers. Cooper and McIntyre focus in particular on the nature and extent of 'commonality' between the perceptions of teachers and pupils. They conclude that there is substantial agreement between teachers and pupils on what effective learning is and what teachers can do to facilitate it. At the same time, they argue that pupils have a clearer and more detailed understanding than their teachers of how particular teaching strategies interact with their learning processes, and that teachers may at times adopt strategies and methods which are not conducive to effective learning. One implication is that teachers could benefit from a greater understanding of the strategies which pupils actually adopt to facilitate their learning.

It is clear that the perceptions of teaching and learning presented in this book have been elicited from a wide range of participants, in a variety of educational contexts, on a number of different topics. This diversity is in itself something to be remarked upon, and even celebrated — at a time when there are widespread fears of an over-riding conformity in our educational system, it is refreshing to be reminded of the richness and complexity of the perceptions held by different participants in that system. At the same time, it is possible to identify a number of common issues or concerns which can be seen to emerge from the different contributions.

The first common concern is essentially methodological: how do we gain access to a person's 'perceptions', and what value do we attach to what we have obtained? As Munn points out in her chapter, perceptions are essentially individual mental phenomena, and yet the main method used to access these perceptions is through language. All the studies reported in this book rely heavily (although by no means exclusively) on interviewing participants, either individually, in pairs, or in small groups. And yet, it is widely recognised that linguistic behaviour can be extremely sensitive to context — what we say to one person in one situation may be very different to what we say to another person in a different situation. A clear example of this comes from Munn's chapter, where she reports virtually no correlation between the ways in which nursery staff talk about children's learning in individual interviews and the comments they make in group discussion. Such observations point unequivocally to the need for obtaining additional evidence from as many different sources as possible, and for caution in interpreting findings based purely on one source of evidence. Both these points are acknowledged either implicitly or explicitly by all the contributors to this volume.

A second and related concern which emerges from several chapters lies in the relationship between perception and action. As a result of the work described here, we have a much greater insight into the perceptions of teaching and learning held by some of the main participants in the educational process, such as teachers, pupils and parents. But what is the relation between these perceptions and their actual practice — as teachers, as learners, and as parents? The question is central to Plewis and Veltman's distinction between the various kinds of 'curriculum' — is what teachers say they are teaching the same as what pupils believe they are being taught? It is also a question raised by the findings reported by Harris and Rudduck — what is the relation between a pupil's attitude to learning, and the amount and quality of learning in which they actually engage? While such questions are in theory open to empirical investigation, in practice the methodology required to answer them is by no means straightforward.

A third issue raised in several chapters is that of the commonality of perceptions. There are two separate questions here. The first concerns the extent to which different participants in the educational process have similar or different perceptions concerning particular aspects of the teaching and learning process. This question is addressed most directly by

Cooper and McIntyre, who suggest that there is substantial commonality between teachers and pupils on some aspects of teaching and learning, but not on others. The question is also addressed by Mitchell, Brumfit and Hooper, who suggest there may be differences between English and foreign language teachers in their perceptions regarding the role of knowledge about language, and by Desforges, Hughes and Holden, who report differences between teachers and parents in their perceptions of the value of assessment. Such differences in perception are perhaps to be expected, although they still need to be explained. The second question concerning commonality is rather different, and concerns the extent to which different participants in the educational process are aware of each others' perceptions — particularly when they differ from their own. Here, our findings are perhaps less expected, and give more cause for concern. Thus it seems from the chapter by Harris and Rudduck that some teachers may not be fully aware of how their pupils regard learning in the early years of secondary school. It also appears from the findings of Desforges, Hughes and Holden that many teachers may be unaware of their parents' views on assessment. Thus one of the main implications to emerge from the research reported in this book is the need for a greater appreciation all round of the different perceptions held by different participants in the educational process.

Finally, a word of caution. The research reported here is still in its early stages. Much more work needs to be done before definitive answers can be provided to the questions which have been raised. Nevertheless, the initial findings of the ESRC research programme have evidently raised a number of interesting and important issues, and indicate that the programme will in due course make a substantial contribution to educational research in Britain.

1 Perceptions of Teaching and Learning in Preschool Centres

PENNY MUNN

Introduction

This chapter presents the view of 'Perceptions of teaching and learning' from the preschool. In Britain, preschools are unique among schools in that there is a great deal said about the learning that occurs within them, but rather less about the teaching that takes place, which is sometimes referred to as 'planning', 'facilitating' 'providing learning opportunities' or other such terms. While it may not be teaching in the didactic sense it is misguided to suggest that learning frequently takes place in the absence of teaching; there is a sense in which preschool teaching has been rendered invisible by not being spoken of.

It is important that we have some understanding of preschool teaching at this time of change. However, the meaning of teaching at this level is not immediately apparent. There are two dictionary senses of the word 'to teach'. One sense of the word means 'to explain or show', while another means 'to impart knowledge'. The first sense points to the person who is being taught while the second points to the knowledge which is being imparted. We don't have two distinct words for these senses of 'teach' because they are not separate. It would be inaccurate to suggest that there is a 'person' aspect and a 'knowledge' aspect of teaching, because teaching is about managing the relation between 'persons' and 'knowledge'. However, there is a sense in which perceptions of (and talk about) teaching may be aligned more to one than another on a person-knowledge dimension.

This seems especially obvious when one takes the case of preschool teaching, where an extreme 'person' sense of teaching is operative. The younger the child, the less the emphasis lies on the knowledge which is taught. Traditionally, preschool education has been concerned with children learning through play, developing their creative potential, establishing friendships with other children, and other such person-centred aims. The knowledge-centred aims of preschool (acquiring cognitive and perceptual skills relevant to the statutory curriculum) are constructed from these more basic person-centred aims. The reason for this state of affairs is not hard to understand. The 'knowledge' sense of teaching emphasises learning outcomes and the outcome of preschool learning is either very mysterious and 'cannot be taught' (as in the acquisition of language) or it is quite trivial (as in the acquisition of physical skills). Before children go to school they need to learn how to button their coats, tie their shoelaces, distinguish shapes and name colours, for instance. These are clearly very important things for small children to learn, but the relation between learning how to do these things in preschool and the curricular goals of primary school is questionable. The traditional solution to the problem of the relation between preschool and school is to extrapolate forwards from basic tasks to later cognitive developments. This is done by pointing to the cognitive content which can be seen in basic tasks and by claiming continuity with later educational products. For example:

- Buttoning up coats involves one-to-one correspondence and therefore maps onto counting.
- Tying shoelaces involves spatial awareness and therefore maps onto mathematical development.
- Distinguishing colours and shapes involves perceptual discrimination and therefore maps onto reading.

By such extrapolation, cognitive aspects of the preschool curriculum are created from basic tasks and an educational discourse is constructed. The links between the preschool and statutory school curriculum exist in teachers' perceptions and in this educational discourse. It is a problematic construction, however, because the learning process is not observable; it can only be inferred, or assumed, or its products measured. It requires knowledge on the part of the teacher to see learning about one-to-one correspondence in the buttoning of a coat. It also requires an act of faith, since teachers get no confirming feedback for their belief that children are learning. It is this 'seeing' of learning in everyday activities that characterises preschool educational discourse; without such extrapolation there is little in preschool that is directly relevant to specific areas of knowledge.

It is rare at this age for children themselves to see their activities as 'educational' and there is therefore very little metacognitive linkage between teacher and child goals. There is no commonality of perception between adult and child about what is being learnt at preschool. At this level the delivery of the curriculum depends very much on the presence of the teacher's perception of why certain activities have a learning content and on the teacher's use of this perception to plan specific learning opportunities. Nursery teachers themselves call this 'having your curriculum up your sleeve', and their opportunistic use of situations is similar to the way in which parents teach young children — the common constraint being the motivational and attentional characteristics of very young children. These arrangements create unique difficulties under current conditions of educational change.

Downward Pressure on the Preschool Curriculum

Recent changes in the primary curriculum (in Scotland, the 5–14 programme) have resulted in downward pressure on preschool provision. The specifically cognitive curricular aims have been highlighted and prior- itised over the more basic aims. Given the structure of preschool curriculum goals outlined above, such pressure should result in marked tensions for preschool practitioners since knowledge-centred aims cannot be prioritised over person-centred aims. The result of such pressure on teachers' practices is predictable: they sense the threat to their own agenda and mount a vigorous defence of traditional nursery practice by shifting various goalposts while retaining the important core concepts. The role of their perceptions of children's learning would be central to this defence and therefore seem worthy of systematic study.

Studying Perceptions of Learning

Staff perceptions of preschool childrens' learning were derived from data from two consecutive research projects into literacy and numeracy practices in preschool. The first project was carried out in 10 Scottish day nurseries. The second project (a systematic comparison of ways of devel- oping staff concepts of children's learning) was carried out in a variety of Scottish preschool establishments. Both projects used interview data and group discussions to examine perceptions of learning and the quality of teaching. There were two methodological problems to this approach. The first was a problem in reliability. Perceptions are individual mental phe- nomena, yet the data were drawn from linguistic images of these phenom- ena. The context dependent and changeable nature of these linguistic images creates problems in ascertaining just what these individual percep- tions are. The second methodological problem was a problem in construct validity. It seems intuitively sensible to assume, given reliable measure- ment of a person's perceptions of learning, that such a measure will tell us something about the quality of teaching and learning initiated by that person. Yet, given the discrepancies that exist between language and action, the relations between adult perceptions of learning and the quality of actual teaching and learning need to be defined empirically. Observational data have been gathered which allow examination of this empirical relation, although these data are not reported in the present chapter. I used the data from the first project (tape-recorded interviews and group discussions) to do a brief phenomenography (Marton, 1988) of concepts of children's learning evident in interviews and discussions from ten Scottish day nurseries. I then used the data from the second project (the data were similar, although more extensive and differently structured) to explore the issues raised concerning teacher perceptions

Data from Non-teachers

In the first project staff were asked:

- How do you help young children learn about number and reading?

The answers were fairly predictable, given that the question focused on action. The most frequent response was a list of activities connected with learning about number or about reading. There was no spontaneous mention of a rationale which underpinned or connected the various activities mentioned, and these responses looked like a sort of 'recipe knowledge'. That is, in response to the question the interviewees produced ideas about their actions, about what they did.

It was not possible to tell from the language sample itself whether such a construction of early literacy and numeracy was actually sufficient to impel suitable action, but the observational data suggested that it was not and that there were considerable discrepancies between what the staff intended and what the children experienced. Some sort of rationale for the elicited 'recipes' might have provided a link between knowledge and action, but there wasn't any way of telling from the responses themselves whether such a rationale was present. In order to discriminate more finely between individuals I looked at the answers to a more open-ended question.

- Could you describe a child who is quick to learn?

This question produced a great deal of variation, in that there were marked individual differences in the language used to describe such a child. Many of the interviewees used language which operated very much at the 'surface' level. They described the products of learning, gave lists of achievements, or simply recounted observable behaviour which was typical of such a child. About one-third of the respondents, however, used language which acknowledged the causes and inner complexity of the children's behaviour. Some of this language could be described as 'inner-state' language; language which went beyond the immediately observable behaviour to describe inferred mental processes. Some of the references were direct references to the processes by which very young children learn; imitation, paying attention, following instructions, listening carefully, exploring.

It is unlikely that those staff members who responded to questions at the level of surface behaviour had no concept of how children learn; rather, their alignment on the person — knowledge dimension of teaching was towards the knowledge rather than towards the person. It is questionable, however, whether it is possible to determine an individual's 'concept of children's learning' from an interview transcript. It may be, for instance, that those respondents who used inner-state language and made reference to learning processes did so simply because they were more articulate.

In order to understand more about the way staff spoke about children's learning I next looked at data from discussion groups formed by these same respondents. The topic of these discussions had been literacy or numeracy related activities carried out by the staff, and the discussions had been repeated after approximately four weeks. There were therefore a lot of spontaneous descriptions of children and activities, and individual differences similar to those that the open-ended interview question had elicited. I looked at (a) whether staff used inner-state references in both interviews and group discussions, and (b) whether there were any changes over time in the extent to which these references were used.

Similarity across contexts

Of the 31 staff originally interviewed, 15 were involved in the discussion groups. The match between style of speech in interview and in discussion context was evaluated by examining the discussion data for references to learning processes or other inner state references. There was no match. Individuals who had used inner-state references during the interviews didn't necessarily use them in discussion, and vice versa. These references were clearly very sensitive to context and it was apparent that affirmation and support between speakers in the group discussion were more important for the use of references to children's learning than any 'inner tendency' on the part of the speaker to use such language. Affirmation and support occur over fairly long stretches of dialogue and consist not only of agreement, but also enquiries as to meaning, invitations to expand topics and the production of similar or matching topics.

Change over time

Examination of patterns of language use over time showed a progression from 'surface level' descriptions of events (actions, length of time spent on task) to more complex descriptions of children's subjectivity (thinking processes, intentions, mental attitudes, what the activities meant to the children). Again, however, there was evidence of sensitivity to social context. These changes occurred only in groups in which speakers gave each other a high degree of affirmation. In groups where such affirmation was not in evidence, speakers seemed almost to defend themselves against such references to children's experiences and no changes were seen in the way they spoke. In groups where the progression did develop, it was as though a consensus as to the underlying topic (the children's subjectivity) was emerging from the group.

Do Conversational Processes Sustain Concepts of Learning?

It appeared, then, that talking about learning processes was an activity which was linked more to conversational 'ambience' than to individual understanding, and that it was only in establishments with a positive 'conversational climate' that extensive discussion of learning processes developed over time. These data raise questions about the role which teachers may play in developing and sustaining concepts of learning in staff working with preschool children. In addition to the role of physically organising the delivery of the curriculum, it is possible that they have an important role in establishing conversation about learning processes. This question was further explored using data from the second project (interviews from head teachers and group discussions with staff). Since the relation between interviews and discussions in these subsequent data were used to draw conclusions, the inconsistency across contexts in the previous dataset requires some explanation.

If we imagine that language is a simple reflection of perception, then these interviews and group discussions had produced contradictory indications of staff perceptions of learning. As Edwards & Potter (1992) point out, however, variance in linguistic data is produced by motivational factors and by the role which language plays in achieving purely social goals. The two situations I drew on for data in the first project had provided the research subjects with very different sets of goals. In the interview situation they were providing generalised accounts of learning and justifications of their actions to an outsider with whom they had no shared experience of working practice. In this situation, the structure and coherence of apparent perceptions of learning depended on the specific questions asked by the interviewer. In the group discussion their goals were more complex in that they were maintaining relationships with fellow-workers as well as producing descriptions and interpretations of particular activities and particular children. These activities and children often constituted experiences which had been shared with others and thus required that a consensual description be constructed. In these situations, the structure and coherence of individual perceptions depended on the affirmation and support of other speakers belonging to the same group. In the second study, then, connections were sought across the two contexts at a rather different level.

Data from Centres with Teachers

During the second project, eight preschool centres are being studied. Data from two of these centres will be used here to illustrate the processes found in centres with teachers. Both centres were nursery schools situated in the same large housing estate outside Glasgow. Both dealt daily with the problems of poverty, poor housing, and negative attitudes towards schooling which were part and parcel of children's lives on this estate.

Teacher perceptions

In order to discover how the heads of these centres saw the role of the nursery in children's learning I asked them

• How does your nursery encourage learning in the children?.

This question elicited fairly lengthy accounts of the way in which learning was planned.

The head of Nursery A gave an account in which the process of learning figured prominently. She mentioned many specific strategies for creating a learning environment for the children. She also spoke of the need to provide a wide variety of carefully planned experiences, and of the adults' responsibility to notice learning opportunities and to intervene where necessary. She saw learning as all-pervading and needing thorough planning, and her estimate of the support staff needed to encourage learning fitted well with this view of learning. She recounted in detail the importance of in-service training for her staff and the particular importance of opportunities to communicate in-service material to the rest of the staff.

The head of Nursery B gave a rather different account of learning in her nursery. She recounted the specific aims and objectives of her planning — viz., to get children to listen, to mix socially and to realise social manners. Her account of how learning was encouraged was also very specific. Nursery workers began by finding out what was needed; they then worked individually and in groups and also enlisted the parents' aid in specific learning objectives. When probed on the support her staff needed to encourage learning, she gave a critical evaluation of her staff's attention to the processes of learning and spoke at length of the methods she used to convey ideas about the learning process. She worked hard to help staff be aware of what the children understood of any activity, and to help them to use notions of evaluation and progression — ideas which she herself used in working with children.

Staff perceptions

In order to discover how staff spoke about children's learning I asked each participating staff member to describe an average three year old, an average four year old, and the difference between them.

Staff from Nursery A spoke in a highly reflective manner about children's learning, making many references to the processes of learning — questions, answers, conversations, understanding, concentration, wanting to know, etc.

The interviews of staff from Nursery B showed a concern with the content of children's learning, and with the details of what was done in a concrete sense to provide learning opportunities. There were virtually no references to learning processes, and none of the reflective statements about children's experiences of learning which had been so evident in the Nursery A staff interviews.

Matches between perceptions

The interviews from these nurseries showed a good 'fit' between what the heads expected of a learning environment and what their staff saw as important aspects of children's learning. In Nursery A, the talk was of process, whereas in Nursery B the talk was very specific and detailed and concerned mainly the content of learning. Whether nursery heads had adapted their mode of talk to their staff's way of thinking, or vice versa, was immaterial; in both nurseries there were ways of talking about learning which appeared to be common to both teachers and their helpers. This suggested that there was some validity to the idea that adult notions of children's learning were constructed during conversations between adults. In order to explore further the construction of notions of children's learning, I looked at how the staff in each of these nurseries spoke about children's learning when they were in conversation with each other. This was done by examining transcripts of discussions held with staff during an intervention which focused the conversation on children's learning.

Discussion in Nursery A

The topics selected for discussion with Nursery A's staff were those related to the adult's role in young children's learning. During discussion, practical examples of goal setting and responsibility transfer were commented on, and their meaning and relevance for children's learning was made explicit. Staff were asked especially to notice similar examples when they happened and to bring these to subsequent discussions. Over the course of time it was to be expected, then, that there would be changes in how children's learning was discussed.

The staff had actually been surprised by the discrepancy between their initial estimate of the children's ability and the degree of difficulty they had seen in the children's reactions. The initial discussion focused very much on the characteristics of the children's performance. One discussant tried to get a child to match some coloured blocks to a photograph of several such blocks showing different orientations:

K: He was very easily distracted all during this. He kept looking round him and talking about other things while I was trying to get him to do this. When eventually he couldn't manage — he couldn't grasp that that was a different position from this. So eventually I showed him the correct position. I pointed out these two were not the same. Then showed him that that was the same position as in the picture. And that that was in the same position as in the picture. Then I asked him — took it away and asked him to do the same again. And he couldn't. What he did was — he put them all like that.

Subsequent discussion focused on the learning processes entailed in the children overcoming difficulties, as in this extract where the same discussant talks about the same child completing a six-piece jigsaw:

K: And he got four pieces in correctly. And the last two pieces he just — he couldn't get it in. So I asked him — aye, that's what he did. He took all the pieces off when he couldn't get the last two pieces in. He just took them off as though he was going to try it again. But he tried to do it on the table — without the board. He put the board to the one side. And he tried to do it on the table. Right. And then he ended up — he couldn't do that either, and he got really mad. And he ended up picking all the pieces up and putting them on top of the board — you know, just on the top. And then putting it back in the cupboard. And then — I told him to take it back and try again. He just got up, pushed it away, and walked away. He just didn't want anything to do with it. He wanted to just go and play. I managed to persuade him to come and sit down again, and I gave him a simpler jigsaw puzzle to do. He managed to do this one right away.

The final discussion developed into a reflective consideration of learning process in which different perceptions of the same child were contrasted.

K: Oh when he was getting ready to go to the sports centre this morning — I was taking four children up to the sports centre this morning — Bob was standing at the — you know the sorting table?

And there'd been teddies out. And he shouted — I can't remember how it was he shouted over — he says right 'What colour is there?' I've never heard him do anything like that before.

E: No, he's picked that up.

K: But he had three red teddies in a line. He can match — he's good at the matching but he doesn't know his colours.

E: And has anybody done that with him?

K: He's never done anything like that before, you know — even worked with — He's usually running about, throwing things about. I've never seen him actually stand and do it himself — like match colours himself. That's the first time I've ever seen him do that.

K: He just keeps — looking all around him. You know he's just — he's looking to see what else he could be doing, while we're doing an activity.

E: Well when I was up your end the other day it was again 'Come and see this' — the things in the catalogue.

K: I'm going to try the next time not a catalogue but a book. Maybe get him to tell me what's in the book.

Changes common to all discussants were an increase in the detail with which children's abilities were described and increasing frequency of positive references to incidents in which children were helped.

Discussion in Nursery B

The topics selected for the discussions with Nursery B's staff were those relating to internal processes in young children's learning. As with Nursery A, practical examples of error reactions, memory constraints, understanding and metacognition were commented on during discussion, and staff were asked especially to notice examples of similar events for future discussion. Just as in Nursery A, one would expect changes over time in the extent to which children's learning was discussed and in the manner of this discussion.

The initial discussion focused on the abilities and non-abilities of the children, as in this example where the first discussant had watched a child trying to do a 9-pieces jigsaw:

E: It was just the fact that she hadn't done it. She's just the type of child that anything that she doesn't want — you know 'I can't do it'. She won't try. But she did do it, and then she was like that — 'Wow I've done it!'. And she did go up and get one out herself. And then she went back to her normal 'I cannae'. I'm going to keep an eye on her anyway because like that — she should be moving on anyway.

M: I think we'll see her chart — it will go up more.

Subsequent discussion focused to a greater extent on the internal processes affecting children, as in the following example concerning a child who was said to be afraid of the computer.

E: I found Craig will go over with his friends. If he sees Charles going over, he'll go over. He'll still not want to go over — if you say to him 'go over' he'll hang back, but he will go over eventually. I think the more you try to push Craig the more he'll stand back and say no.

The final discussion developed into a conversation about specific techniques used to deflect processes adversely affecting children's progress, as in the following discussion of an ambivalent child:

E: She's one of these children that I used to say, like 'Come on, do this jigsaw'. No way. I mean, it was self-defeating. 'I will not do it. I can't do it' it was.

M: This was fear of the unknown kind of thing?

E: Fear of the unknown. And as soon as you walked away and left her, there she would sit down and do it.

It was notable that there was considerable agreement and convergence in this final discussion — a conversational process quite different from the reflective contrasts seen in Nursery A.

Differences between nurseries in patterns of conversation

In these two nurseries there were clear differences in the ways of talking about children's learning which were evident in both interviews and group discussions. Nursery A focused on process while Nursery B focused on product and practice. The difference in the group discussions, however, lay not so much in the level at which learning was discussed, since both staff groups engaged in discussion of abstraction and process, as in the conversational processes which operated to create the discussion. In Nursery A the discussion of learning developed into a reflective thinking aloud in which different points of view about the same children were contrasted and compared. The discussants almost seemed to relish the different positions they were adopting, and there were instances of discussants adopting positions, changing position, and then reverting back to the first position.

In Nursery B the conversational processes creating the final discussion were based on agreement and construction of common experience rather than on differentiation and contrast. In this nursery, discussants constructed the topic around the practices which they adopted in specific situations. Cooperative processes of topic-construction were much in evidence, even where discussants disagreed with each other.

How Important are Teacher Perceptions in Establishing Conversation about Children's Learning?

Whereas discussion of children's learning had only developed under optimal conversational conditions in the establishments without teachers, in both of these nurseries from the second sample discussion of learning situations developed very quickly over time. This suggested that the existence of an established discourse of learning (assumed to be related to the presence of the teacher) is an important and constant factor in the establishment of this kind of discourse. There were large differences between the two nurseries in the content of the discussions that developed, linked with quite striking differences between the head teacher's accounts of how they encouraged learning, which were in turn linked with initial differences in the way staff talked about children's learning.

Conclusion

Although no firm conclusions may be drawn from the data presented here, since the work is still in progress, discourses of children's learning do seem to be a function of group or institutional communication as well as of individual cognitions. The practical questions about such discourses concern their effects on children's learning. Teaching and learning are clearly very different from talking about teaching and learning, and it would be useful to know whether ways of talking about learning are associated with the learning experiences that children actually have. Further study of the nurseries in the present sample will address issues concerning the relation of these patterns of talk to the children's learning experiences. Questions about responses to downward pressure from changes in the primary curriculum will also be addressed through analysis of variation between establishments on a number of variables.

References

Edwards, D. and Potter, J. (1992) *Discursive Psychology*. London: Sage.
Marton, F. (1988) Phenomenography: A research approach to investigating different understandings of reality. In R. Sherman and R. Webb (eds) *Qualitative Research in Education: Focus and Methods*. London: Falmer Press.

2 Teachers' Reports of Curriculum Coverage in Response to Change

IAN PLEWIS and MARIJCKE VELTMAN

Introduction

This chapter provides an introduction to some of the conceptual, operational and methodological issues raised by the project known as CECIL (Classroom Experiences of Children in Inner London). The project as a whole has several aims which include:

(1) measuring change (since the mid-1980s) in

    (a) the coverage of the maths curriculum in Years 1 and 2;

    (b) the ways in which pupils in Year 2 classes spend their school day;

and

(2) considering the extent to which Year 1 and 2 classes are grouped for maths, the stability of these groups, the bases on which they are formed, and the relation between grouping, curriculum coverage and pupil progress.

In this chapter we concentrate on pupils' coverage of the maths curriculum. As data collection has only recently started, no results are available yet.

The origins of this research can be found in work carried out at the Thomas Coram Research Unit (TCRU) during the 1980s, firstly in the detailed longitudinal study of a cohort of pupils entering 33 multi-ethnic Inner London infant schools in 1982, described in Tizard *et al.* (1988), and secondly in a project which concentrated on Years 1 and 2 for the cohort entering the same schools in 1986 (Plewis, 1991). We use the term 'curriculum coverage' in this chapter, just as we did in the research referred to above. The term is not, however, standard and other researchers, referring to essentially the same concept, use 'content coverage' (Barr & Dreeben, 1983) and 'opportunity to learn' (Postlethwaite, 1986). We use teacher reports to measure curriculum coverage, and operationalise it as a weighted sum of responses, provided by the teacher for each pupil in her class, to a set of items taken to represent the maths curriculum. Included within the instrument are items such as understanding zero, ordering numbers, and using and recording non-standard measures for length. The weights reflect the relative difficulty of each item; the lower the proportion of pupils experiencing an item, the higher the weight. A detailed description of how the original measure was developed and used can be found in Farquhar *et al.* (1987).

The main results from the earlier work were as follows. First, it was found that, for all three infant school years, about half the overall variation in maths curriculum coverage was between classes, and about half between pupils within classes. In other words, there was substantial differentiation of the maths curriculum within classes, but also pupils' experiences differed considerably depending on which class they happened to be in. Second, Tizard *et al.* (1988) found no consistent differences in the level of maths coverage between their four main groups of interest, i.e. black (Afro-Caribbean) and white boys and girls. Third, both studies found that curriculum coverage was associated with pupil progress, with Plewis (1991) finding evidence to support the idea that some of the variation between classes in pupils' progress can be accounted for by between class differences in curriculum coverage.

The main focus of CECIL is on change over time at the *macro*, or aggregate, level. In other words, we are looking at change or trends across cohorts of pupils, rather than developmentally over age within a cohort, as Tizard *et al.* did. In particular, we would like to find out:

(1) Whether Year 1 and Year 2 pupils are covering more of the maths curriculum now than they were ten years ago — the question of *level*.
(2) Whether there has been a change in the variance of the measure over time, both between classes and between pupils within classes — the question of *variability*.
(3) Whether there is any variation now in maths coverage between the four ethnic/gender groups in a way there was not before — the question of *equal opportunity to learn*.

By going back to a sample of the same schools that were in the original TCRU studies, we hope to be able to answer these questions.

Sample

Our sample of 22 schools are spread across seven Local Education Authorities in Inner London. All the sample schools, but very few of the teachers, had been in the Tizard *et al.* study. Eighteen of the schools have straight Year 1 classes and 4 schools have mixed Year 1 and Year 2 classes. We questioned 28 teachers who provided data on the maths curriculum covered by each of 564 Year 1 pupils.

Measuring Curriculum Coverage

We adapted the curriculum coverage instrument used in the earlier research in order to incorporate the National Curriculum for maths at Key Stage One (KS1) as set out in National Curriculum Council (1991). Kelly (1990) observes that the systematisation of subject knowledge in the National Curriculum represents a version of the curriculum which is sharply at variance with that which has been adopted in primary schools over the last three decades. However, our breakdown of some of the infant curriculum into maths and language in the 1980s research, if perhaps at odds with practice then, nevertheless now provides us with a great opportunity to look at change.

One problem we faced when trying to incorporate the National Curriculum into our curriculum coverage instrument was that it is difficult to assess how teachers actually interpret the National Curriculum guidelines on maths, how important they find certain topics rather than others, and hence how we could condense the National Curriculum into a user-friendly form for teachers to enable them to tell us what was being covered during Years 1 and 2 in maths. As Alexander (1992) points out, teachers use different labels for the same area and frequently one area subsumes another.

As different teaching methods and materials are adopted by schools, another question to consider is how teachers actually translate the National Curriculum into how they teach, and subsequently into what each pupil actually gets taught, or, perhaps more realistically, is given the opportunity to learn. Gehrke *et al.* (1992) put it rather succinctly when they state that 'the act of teaching shapes what is taught, and what is to be taught shapes how it is taught'. The problematic nature of what is taught becomes increasingly apparent. It includes not only how things are taught, such as the relationships and interactions between teachers and pupils, but also many features that characterise what really goes on in schools and classrooms, not the least of which are content and subject matter, and the way these are organised.

To begin to understand what goes on in schools and classrooms, Goodlad *et al.* (1979) assert that it requires appraising such features as intended goals and objectives, learning activities, use of human and material resources, use of time and space, grouping patterns, and assessment of learning. But from whose point of view are these appraisals made? When we ask what schools *really* teach whose opinions are we seeking? The very nature of the curriculum suggests a mixture of perceptions and interpretations accumulating in what teachers say they do, what pupils say they get taught and what 'neutral' observers see gets taught. The influence of national, local, and school policies, adopted textbooks, the interpretations and inferences made by reviewers of curriculum documents and of similar documents in use in classrooms, and assessment procedures, must be added to the overall picture. Also, given the supposed influence of experts such as the curriculum theorists and the subject matter specialists, along with the educational reformers, then the analyses and interpretations of what the curriculum *should* be must also be added to what the curriculum supposedly is.

However, here we are concerned with just three aspects of the curriculum as set out by Gehrke *et al.* (1992). The first is the *planned curriculum*, now represented by the National Curriculum and its guidelines, textbooks, and ultimately teachers' ideas as they formulate what they will do. The second is the *enacted curriculum* by the teachers in the classroom (although there is a problem about whose account of enactment to believe). Third comes the curriculum as experienced by pupils; this is the *experienced curriculum* which is not fully captured either by the planning or by the enactment.

So our task in updating the maths curriculum coverage instrument was to incorporate aspects of the form used for Year 1, and the separate form for Year 2, from the original studies, in order to be able to make comparisons with the present study, and to add to these topics from the National Curriculum for maths which also needed to be in such an instrument to make it valid in the current situation. In other words, we attempted to interpret the National Curriculum for maths in such a way as to anticipate what schools would be teaching, hoping that the way in which we, as researchers, interpreted the planned maths curriculum would not prove too divergent from how schools and teachers interpreted and enacted the National Curriculum. The way in which we set out to establish what the experienced curriculum was for each pupil was through the *teachers'* perceptions of what had been covered rather than from the pupils' point of view.

Hence, our curriculum coverage instrument for the present study is an amalgamation of what the researchers in the earlier studies thought was being taught in maths in the 1980s to infant classes; what the National Curriculum now stipulates should be taught at KS1; and how we as researchers interpreted the National Curriculum and incorporated that into the curriculum coverage instrument. Inevitably, the form we have developed is longer than either of the two forms used in the 1980s work. For example, for Year 1, we now have 131 separate items whereas there were just 43 in the earlier studies, although some of this expansion can be explained by the fact that we now have just one form covering both Years 1 and 2.

There are two versions of the form. One is a 'teacher form' on which the teacher indicates what has been covered in maths during that year by them with at least one pupil in the class, and on this form the teacher is able to state why a particular topic has not been covered. The reasons a teacher can give are:

(a) because they don't teach that particular task;
(b) because they do teach that task but it is too difficult as yet;
(c) because they have not got round to teaching that task yet, not because it is too difficult.

The second version of the form is the individual 'pupil form'. The teacher is asked to complete a form for each pupil in their class in order to identify what each pupil has been given the opportunity to learn in maths. This is not necessarily what they have actually learnt, only what has been covered with that pupil. On the pupil form, the teacher is not asked why a particular topic or task had not been covered by that pupil. One of the strengths of our approach is that we do not assume, as researchers in the past have done, that all pupils in the class have covered the same topics. Such an assumption continues to be unrealistic for English infant schools.

Grouping

There has been little systematic study of grouping in English primary schools — its prevalence, its purpose, its dynamics and its effectiveness (although see Galton & Williamson, 1992). Consequently, it will be impossible to ascertain whether the effects of the Education Reform Act have been to change the prevalence of grouping, and the bases on which groups are formed. It has been suggested that the requirements of the National Curriculum will lead to less grouping and more whole class instruction, but it could also lead to an increase in grouping at the expense of individualised teaching.

Here we are interested in the links between grouping and curriculum coverage, and hence in the association with pupil progress. Wilkinson (1988) characterises such questions as being part of the sociological tradition in research on classroom grouping, as opposed to the sociolinguistic, process-product and cooperative learning traditions. We expect to find that most within class variation in curriculum coverage will be variation between groups within classes, particularly where teachers create groups on the basis of perceived ability. If curriculum coverage is causally related to progress, then, if our expectation is correct, it is important to discover the mechanisms underlying group formation — the links with prior attainment, with age and, especially relevant to issues of equal opportunities, with ethnic group and gender. One simple model is given as Figure 2.1: groups are determined by teachers' assessments of pupils' abilities and possibly also by ethnic group, gender and age; grouping determines the amount of curriculum coverage, with 'high' groups covering more than 'low' groups, and this in turn affects progress. However, progress could also be directly influenced by ethnic group, gender and age (because of differences in teacher behaviour and different home circumstances). This is a within class model which proposes that the previously observed correlation between curriculum coverage and progress can be accounted for by teachers' perceptions, as revealed by their grouping arrangements. A between class model, suggested by Plewis (1991), hypothesises that pupils make more progress in classes that are grouped because more of the curriculum is covered in such classes, and there is a closer match between coverage and ability. Taken together, these two models imply that pupils make more progress in classes that are grouped for maths, and pupils in the 'highest' groups make most progress of all. However, the reality of

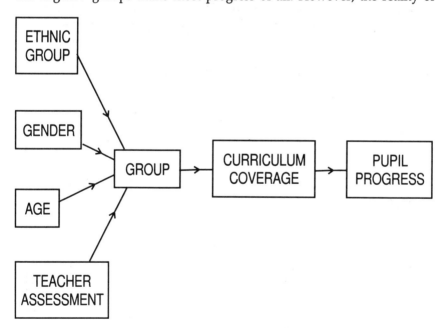

Figure 2.1 Within class model of how grouping might influence pupil progress

classroom grouping may be rather more diverse, and less clear cut, than is being suggested here.

Measuring Change

As we have seen, the focus of the research is on measuring change. However, although the questions are easy to state, it is much more difficult to find valid answers, both to questions about the existence of change and, especially, about the reasons for it. The available data on curriculum change can be represented by Figure 2.2. There are three perspectives on change for these data. The first is developmental, represented by the horizontal boxes, looking at change over age or school year within a cohort as we did for the 1982 cohort, and as we will be able to do in a more limited way with the CECIL cohort. The second looks at secular trends across cohorts within age as represented by the vertical boxes. The third looks at secular trends in developmental changes, as represented by the two hatched boxes. As noted earlier, we are especially interested in secular trends.

As we have seen, our measures of curriculum coverage are not *identical* over time although it is hoped that they are *appropriate* for each cohort. Nevertheless, in a situation where the items making up the overall measure change and, even for the same items, the weights (representing the relative

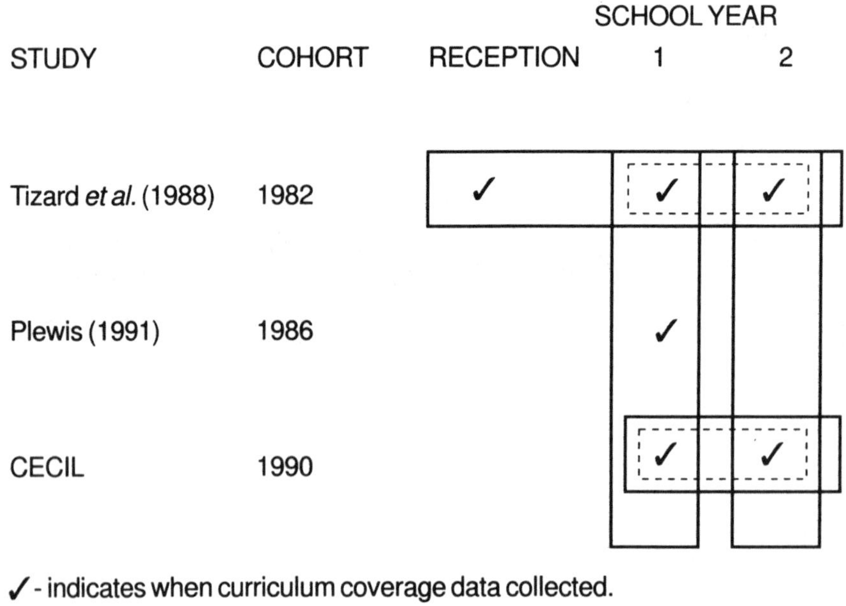

| | | | SCHOOL YEAR | |
STUDY	COHORT	RECEPTION	1	2
Tizard *et al.* (1988)	1982	✓	✓	✓
Plewis (1991)	1986		✓	
CECIL	1990		✓	✓

✓ - indicates when curriculum coverage data collected.

Figure 2.2 Types of change

difficulty) can change, it will not be easy to make statements about absolute change. The difficulty is analogous to the one faced by those wishing to make inferences about changing levels of, for example, reading attainment over time. Reading tests should change as the curriculum changes, and the difficulty level of each item also changes. Consequently, we are never quite sure whether an observed change in mean test scores is due to a change in the instrument or to a genuine change in the population. We can look at individual items, we can correlate the old and new parts of the instrument, and we can see whether there are substantial changes in the weights, but we can never totally escape from this dilemma. Conclusions about relative change are, however, less problematic than they are for aggregate change. With just a few reasonable assumptions, we can, for example, say whether change has been greater for boys than it has for girls, so our questions about equal opportunities can be answered more easily.

References

Alexander, R. (1992) *Policy and Practice in Primary Education*. London: Routledge.

Barr, R. and Dreeben, R. (1983) *How Schools Work*. Chicago: University of Chicago Press.

Farquhar, C., Blatchford, P., Burke, J., Plewis, I. and Tizard, B. (1987) Curriculum diversity in London infant schools. *British Journal of Educational Psychology 59*, 19–30.

Galton, M. and Williamson, J. (1992) *Group Work in the Primary Classroom*. London: Routledge.

Gehrke, N.J., Knapp, M.S. and Sirotnik, K.A. (1992) In search of the school curriculum. In G. Grant (ed.) *Review of Research in Education* Vol. 18. Washington: American Educational Research Association.

Goodlad, J.L. and associates (1979) *Curriculum Inquiry: The Study of Curriculum Practice*. New York: McGraw-Hill.

Kelly, A.V. (1990) *The National Curriculum: A Critical Review*. London: Paul Chapman.

National Curriculum Council (1991) *Consultation Report: Mathematics*. York: National Curriculum Council.

Plewis, I. (1991) Using multilevel models to link educational progress with curriculum coverage. In S. W. Raudenbush and J. D. Willms (eds) *Schools, Classrooms and Pupils: International Studies of Schooling from a Multilevel Perspective*. San Diego: Academic Press.

Postlethwaite, T.N. (ed.) (1986) *International Educational Research: Papers in Honor of Torsten Husen*. Oxford: Pergamon.

Tizard, B., Blatchford, P., Burke, J., Farquhar, C. and Plewis, I. (1988) *Young Children at School in the Inner City*. Hove: Lawrence Erlbaum.

Wilkinson, L.C. (1988) Grouping children for learning: Implications for kindergarten education. In E.Z. Rothkopf (ed.) *Review of Research in Education* Vol.15. Washington: American Educational Research Association.

3 Parents' and Teachers' Perceptions of Assessment at Key Stage 1

CHARLES DESFORGES, MARTIN HUGHES and CATHIE HOLDEN

Introduction

The educational aspiration behind public, standardised, summative assessment (PSSA) procedures is that they (and their attendant syllabuses) set clear standards, promote equity of experience and provide an important impetus for achievement. The products (grades and certificates) are taken to have validity: they are objective evidence of attainment. Unfortunately, research evidence suggests that PSSA techniques, especially where the scores are 'high stakes' (i.e. have high public profile and material consequences) tend to foster narrowed curriculum experience, or 'teaching to tests' (Desforges, 1992). The consequences have been shown to be detrimental to the quality of learning, especially for low attainers (Paris *et al.*, 1991).

Recently, legislators in England and Wales have apparently set aside this track record. Implicitly PSSA has been conceived not as an idea that has failed but as an idea that has not been thoroughly tried. The Government has placed PSSA within a thoroughgoing market philosophy of education in which parents are cast as consumers who will choose amongst traders (schools) on the basis of market information (test scores and other indices such as truancy rates). With, ostensibly at least, parental rights to choose schools, the movement of children is directly correlated with the movement of resources under LMS arrangements. In this approach the publication of PSSA results is the catalyst which will set forces in motion to enhance standards of attainment.

This is an interesting theory based on a large number of untested — and largely unarticulated — assumptions about markets in general and about parental views and actions as 'consumers of education' in particular. The very rapid implementation of recent educational legislation has afforded

26

an opportunity for the empirical exploration of how assessment works in practice in the exchanges between teachers and parents. The research reported here focuses on some aspects of these processes.

Rationale

Part of the expressed impetus behind the 1988 Education Act was that schooling had been 'producer captured' and that it should be given (or given back?) to the consumers where a market philosophy deems it rightly belongs. Explicit here is the view that parents know what they want from their children's schooling and they will be able to see this realised (or not) in certain objective indices notably, in this instance, in achievement scores.

Teachers,in this model, would learn what their customers wanted, presumably through talking about the quality of the goods, and then strive to make their products increasingly marketable. Schools which could not do this would cease to trade: their customers would go elsewhere. These assumptions teased out from a market philosophy have in part informed the design of the present study. They are set out somewhat starkly in Figure 3.1.

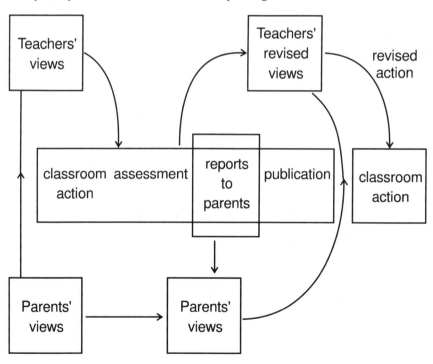

Figure 3.1 Parental influence on teachers' classroom action

Of course these assumed processes of mutual perception between teachers and parents proceed in a wider and complex world of other 'producer' and 'consumer' interests but sufficient is shown here to identify some of our research questions. We have asked, for example, what are teachers' and parents' views of teaching, learning, assessment and standards? What do they understand of each others' views? How do these views relate to teaching and parenting practices? How have their views changed as a consequence of the experience of the first round of SATs in 1991? In this chapter, we focus on the parents' and teachers' views of PSSA with particular reference to the 1991 SATs. Our aim here is to consider what teachers' and parents' views were of SATs and SAT publication before and after experience of SATs. We also consider the degree to which teachers are sensitive to parents' perceptions on these matters.

Method

Twenty Year 2 teachers were recruited representing a range of classroom settings (urban/rural; large school/small school; white/ethnic minority). In each class six 'target' children (3 boys and 3 girls) were selected to represent the attainment range. The parents ($N = 120$) of these children were invited to take part in the project. Parents and teachers were individually interviewed in the Spring before the introduction of SATs in 1991 and in the Summer after the teachers had reported SAT results to parents. As part of a large structured interview they were asked what they knew about SATs, what they felt about them, what value they thought SATs would be (had been) and whether they felt whole school SAT results should be published. Teachers were asked where they thought parents stood on this issue and whether parents needed/wanted to know more or wanted to be involved in pupil assessment. Reciprocally, parents were asked about the degree to which they felt they needed to know more or wanted to be involved. All interviews were tape recorded and responses were allowed to run free. They were subsequently coded into categories derived from the data.

Results

Teachers' views before and after SATs

In Spring 1991, 13 of the 20 teachers in the sample were totally opposed to SATs. Only one teacher was entirely in favour and the remaining six had 'mixed feelings'. Typically, the teachers commented that SATs would narrow the curriculum, that teachers would have to teach to the tests, that teaching would become teacher-centred rather than child-centred, that children's interests and energy would be lost, that the tests would put too much pressure on children through parental anxiety, and that the tests were too vague, badly thought out and no use to children's learning. It was widely felt that children of 7 were too young to be tested, and that the whole procedure belittled the teachers' professional judgement. Typical comments were as follows:

> I just feel they will prove very little... I don't think it will be an accurate record. It's time that's wasted.

> I cannot see the point of testing 7 year olds. They're just too young... They haven't covered half the stuff they're going to be tested on, and these children have the added disadvantage of the language problem.

> It will be difficult for teachers not to teach with tests and results specifically in mind.

Seventeen of the 20 teachers strongly objected to the publication of SATs results. They were virtually unanimous in considering that publishing the results of a whole school was too crude a measure of a school's performance, that the results were open to misinterpretation, that they were unfair to schools in not taking into account the schools' catchment area, and that publication ran the risk of creating poor expectations of some schools and children. For example:

> This school has the best reputation in the area as a friendly caring school but this cannot be ranked. Schools should not be judged only on academic achievement.

> Schools with a high proportion of children without English as their home language would be at a disadvantage. It re-emphasises the racist view that a school with children from different ethnic backgrounds will have lower standards, and that's not necessarily true.

When the teachers were re-interviewed in the Summer of 1991, after they had reported the SATs results to parents, some teachers had changed their views, although the majority had not. Fifteen of the teachers said they stood by their earlier view in regard to SATs as such, three had become more negative about the procedures, and two had become more positive. In regard to publishing results 18 of the teachers retained their initial opinion, one had become more negative and one had become more positive. Those teachers who had changed their views are illustrated by the following comments:

> I have become much more aware of what children can and can't do. It's made me look at them more carefully.

If I felt they (the SATs) had helped the development of the child I wouldn't be so worried. A few were useful. The others were a complete waste of time.

I think I feel a little more strongly against publication (of results) now. Many of our decisions have been subjective and if one wanted to, one could slant the results one way or the other.

Parents' views before and after SATs

There were 120 parents in the sample. In the Spring, 51% of them felt that SATs were a good idea. A further 14% were generally positive but with some reservations. 21% were negative about SATs. That being said, only 6% had a fairly clear idea of what the SATs involved, 29% had misconceptions or only partial understanding, and 63% said they had little or no understanding of what was involved.

Parents in favour of SATs mentioned that they would help teachers to identify and remediate weaknesses (28% mentioned this), and that early assessment was especially important (16%). Parental reservations expressed included the view that children of 7 were too young to be tested (18%), that there was a danger of early labelling (12%) and that SATs put too much pressure on children (19%). The arguments for and against SATs are illustrated by the following comments:

It's all part of going to school, isn't it? They go to school to learn and you want to know if they're learning anything or not, so you can help them.

It can show if something's wrong with the teacher or the school, or if you've got to put more into your child's education.

It's a total waste of time, energy and money. It will not help children in any way. Teachers will end up just teaching to the state test and nothing more… The loss of teaching time will lower standards.

I'm happy to rely on the teacher's own awareness. There's enough pressure on teaching and this assessment may take time away from class teaching.

In regard to publishing the school's results 37% of parents thought this was a good idea and a further 6% supported this view with minor reservations. 32% had no strong feelings on the matter whilst 25% were against the idea. Positive comments in regard to publication included the views that it would help parents to compare schools (mentioned by 23% of all parents), that it would help parents to judge if schools were up to standard (24%) and that it would lead to schools working harder (12%). Reservations included the views that it would lead to unprofitable competition (9%) and would be damaging (14%). There were large numbers of other reservations but none mentioned by more than 10% of parents in the sample. Typical comments were:

> Our school has had a bad name, because of its location, and we would like to prove people wrong. It's a good school and people should be told...

> It would give you some idea of how the children at a particular school have done... It depends what use is made of the information. If the teachers are happy with it, then that's fine.

> This is a bad thing — it will put more pressure on children and teachers... You won't get a happy relationship then.

> I don't agree with it. It's a personal thing. Children are so different — the range of children is so vast in this one year.

After the experience of SATs and reporting to the parents, 98% of the sample acknowledged that they had received a written report. 65% said they understood the report, although 23% said they didn't understand the levels. 80% of parents said they were pleased with the report. What did parents now think about SATs and the publication of results?

69% of parents said they had not changed their views. Of these, 14% said they held the same view but felt they were better informed and more reflective about the matter. 17% (20 parents) had changed their view. Of these, six parents had become negative and ten had become positive about testing. Reservations mentioned by the sample at this point included 'SATs told us nothing new' (21%) 'teachers comments were more helpful' (9%) 'too much stress for teachers' (12%) and 'SATs restricted Summer teaching' (9%). Positive comments included 'we now know where to help' (15%). In regard to publication 85% said they had not changed their position. 18 parents had changed their mind amongst whom eight had become more negative about the idea. Some of these points are illustrated by the following two parents, whose views changed but in opposite directions:

> I've changed my mind...children get nervous and you judge them and it's wrong. Just before summer we received written reports. Everyone wanted to see other children's results... It was very difficult for me...and for parents whose child didn't do so well. Another lady said 'my son didn't do well — its because I'm uneducated'.

> It's good the way they've done it... I'm more likely to help with reading at home... (I know now) the subjects he's best at... I never had comments like that before.

The attitudes held before the SATs by the parents and teachers towards SATs and the publication of results are summarised in Table 3.1.

Table 3.1 Attitude of teachers and parents towards SATs and publication of results

Attitude before SATs	to SATS		to publication	
	Teachers (actual)	Parents (%)	Teachers (actual)	Parents (%)
In favour	1	65	0	43
Against	13	21	17	25
Mixed	6	14	3	32

Tested by X^2 both these distributions indicate that teachers are significantly more negative and parents are significantly more positive ($p < 0.001$) in regard to these matters.

In general we can say that in our samples, parents were more positive about SATs and the publication of results than teachers, and that both parties had fewer reservations about SATs than about publication. Where benefits could be seen they were more likely to refer to the support of individual children than to the judgement of schools, although at least 1 in 5 of parents saw the latter as an advantage of publication.

Table 3.2 Parents' views and teachers' perceptions of those views (Spring 1991)

Issue	% of Teachers (N=20) suggesting 'parents view'	Parents' (N=120) % 'expressed view'
What do parents know about assessment?	80% of teachers said 'very little'	63% of parents said 'very little'
Where do parents get their information from?	35% 'school meetings' 30% 'class teachers' 90% 'media'	19% 'school' 15% 'teacher' 20% 'media'
Do parents want to know more?	35% 'no' 20% 'a few' 35% 'most or all'	91% 'yes'
Do parents want to be involved in assessment?	40% 'no' 15% 'a few' 40% 'don't know'	21% 'no' 38% 'yes' 25% 'yes depending'
What do parents feel about assessment?	15% 'against' 25% 'no idea' 40% 'parents don't know enough to have an opinion'.	21% 'against' 65% 'in favour' 14% 'mixed feelings'
What do parents feel aboutpublication of results?	35% 'against' 15% 'in favour' 45% 'don't know'	25% 'against' 43% 'in favour' 32% 'mixed feelings'

Teachers' perceptions of parents' views

Recall that the machinery of the 1988 Act was in part intended to require teachers to become more sensitive to parents' views and desires. How well do teachers 'read' parents on the matter of assessment? Table 3.2 compares parents' actual views with teachers' perceptions of those views on the central questions we raised.

Table 3.2 indicates there are some areas of major discrepancy between teachers' perceptions of parents' views and what parents actually think. For example 91% of the parents said they wanted to know more about assessment, but only 35% of the teachers felt that 'most' or 'all' of the parents wanted to know more. Nor was the situation improved by the actual experience of SATs. For example, by the Summer of 1991, and after the experience of SATs, reporting to parents and discussing the reports, 20% of the teachers said they had 'no idea' whether parents were in favour of assessment, 25% felt that most parents were negative about assessment, 25% felt most were indifferent and 25% said they had insufficient knowledge on which to base a judgement. In contrast, it will be recalled that at least 65% of parents were generally in favour of SATs.

Discussion

The sample of teachers in this study was only 20. It would be foolish to overgeneralise. Added to that caution there are technical difficulties in interpreting these data. Whilst we can be confident that we have the teachers' and the parents' own views, getting mutual perceptions is more difficult. The teachers were asked to comment on the views of the parents they were familiar with. Even so this amounts to asking them to generalise somewhat. The teachers did not claim to find this difficult but we cannot be certain here quite which parents the teachers are referring to when they state their view of the parents' view.

With these cautions in mind perhaps the most striking features of our data so far are as follows. First, there are important differences between teachers and parents in their attitudes to assessment and publication. As we saw in Table 3.1, the teachers were significantly more negative than parents both to SAT assessment and to the publication of results. Put simply, the main difference is that the parents tended to think that these procedures might generate useful information, while the teachers did not.

The second important feature of our data concerns teachers' perceptions of parents' views. It is one thing for traders to have different views from their customers, but it is another for traders to be unaware of their customers' tastes. The data reported in Table 3.2 suggest just such a situation in regard to SATs. 40% of the sample of teachers did not know whether parents wanted to be involved in assessment or what parents felt about the publication of results. Only 1 in 3 teachers said that most or all parents wanted to know more about assessment, yet 91% of parents claimed that this was something they were interested in. Other differences of misinterpretation are evident in Table 3.2.

There are problems in interpreting these data. There was certainly no antipathy between teachers and parents. As indicated, 80% of parents were well pleased with the outcomes of the reporting season. It is possible that parents told teachers one thing (or nothing) and told our interviewers something else. Saying that one is not interested in assessment might be taken as being not interested in one's child. On the other hand, according to the teachers, meetings had been held on assessment to which, by and large, parents had not turned up. A number of interpretations are possible of this, including that the meetings were held at awkward times, or that parents are more interested in their own child's progress than in the formal mechanics of assessment.

The findings reported here represent only the first stage of our project. They raise issues which we intend to pursue further with subsequent cohorts of parents and teachers. We hope that further reports of our findings will allow a fuller and more detailed analysis of these issues.

References

Desforges, C. (1992) Assessment and learning *Forum* 34 (3), 68–9.
Paris, S.G., Lawton, T.A., Turner, J.C. and Roth, J.L. (1991) A development perspective on standardised achievement testing. *Educational Researcher* 20 (5), 12–17.

4 'School's Great — Apart From the Lessons': Students' Early Experiences of Learning in Secondary School

SUSAN HARRIS and JEAN RUDDUCK

Introduction

This chapter is written from data gathered during the first year of a longitudinal study involving three schools.[1] The study is called 'Making Your Way Through Secondary School: Students and their Learning'. The research is designed to provide insight into the experience of being a secondary school student in the 1990s. 'School career' is a key concept — 'the sociological equivalent of the psychological notion of child "development"' (Waterhouse, 1992: 9). The value of the concept of career, as Goffman (1961: 119) explains, is its 'two-sidedness': one side is linked to such things as 'image of self and self-identity' while the other concerns the relationship of the individual to the 'institutional complex'. Hence, students' school careers can be looked at not only in terms of movement through the year cohorts of the school — each ostensibly carrying new demands and offering turning points — but also in terms of students' changing experience of the school and the meanings attached to relationships with peers and teachers.

The research is being conducted in three comprehensive schools — one in each of three LEAs. It is interview-based and concentrates on one group of students in each school who were 12 years old (Y8) at the start of the research and who will be 16 years at the end. The interview data are contextualised through information gathered from teachers as well as through the analysis of school records and documents.

We identified schools that were reasonably buoyant in terms of student numbers and generally confident about their approach and their future. The schools were interestingly different and were facing the challenge of change in ways that reflected their particular contexts and histories. One school has an economically, socially and culturally diverse student population. One school serves a predominantly disadvantaged, working class and ethnically mixed community but has a small new influx of white middle class parents. The third school is predominantly white and working class and serves an economically disadvantaged area where unemployment is high.

After the headteachers had confirmed their interest in the project, each school managed the task of consulting/informing staff, governors, parents and students in ways that were consistent with its preferred style. In each school it was agreed that one Year 8 class (average size, 28 students) would be selected for participation in the study. In all three schools Y8 classes were organised on mixed ability lines.

In each academic year three rounds of interviews are carried out with students (in the first year they were interviewed in pairs, thereafter individually). Subject teachers working with the target class are interviewed once a year, while the form tutor of the target class, the headteacher and other senior members of staff are interviewed two or three times a year. Student interviews last approximately 25 minutes while teacher interviews are usually about 30 minutes long. All interviews are tape-recorded and later transcribed and stored on computer. In addition, the researchers attend occasional key events affecting their target group (such as options evening or parents' evening). Three researchers are involved, each responsible for gathering data in one school.[2]

We are part way through a four year study and this chapter offers only a general and provisional review of some themes looked at across the three schools without attempting to differentiate the schools in any systematic way. The two themes which we focus on — membership and labelling — have been well documented in other research (Beynon, 1985; Furlong, 1976; Pollard, 1985; Woods, 1980, 1981), but what we attempt to do here is to explore how these themes relate to learning in the early years of secondary schooling.

Emphasising Learning: The Experience of 'New' Students

Recent educational reform, which has seen increased parental choice, encouraged opting out and fostered the publication of league tables, has increased pressure on schools to be seen to 'deliver the goods'. On the face of it there does not seem to be anything particularly problematic about defining the school as a place of learning. But how do teachers welcome new students into the school as a learning community and how do they signal the seriousness of learning? Our data suggest that during the early period of secondary schooling, despite the best efforts of schools, students are unlikely to experience classroom learning as the central feature of school life.

Earlier studies of transition have shown that for students the move from primary to secondary school is complex and demanding. There are many things on students' minds other than learning: getting to know the new school — the buildings, the surroundings, the areas they are allowed in and those that are barred; they have to get used to new faces — different students, different teachers — and much more movement between classes (Measor & Woods, 1984; Beynon, 1985; Cullingford, 1991). In 1984, Measor & Woods identified five sources of students' anxiety on transfer to their secondary school: the size of the school; the discipline/authority system; the work demands; the fear of being bullied; and the fear of losing friends. The students we interviewed shared many of these concerns. They were also anxious about having to adapt to a new social position as a member of the youngest group in the school rather than the oldest; and they were anxious about their academic position: those who had been 'top' in their primary schools were worried about whether they would maintain this position in their new school, and those who had 'messed around a bit' in their primary school hoped that there would be a chance for a fresh start in their secondary school.

While many schools are now increasing the support they provide to help students cope with the disorientations of transition, teachers may not always realise how complex this experience is from the students' perspective. Indeed, some staff commented that they had, until now, believed that once their induction programme for new students was over they would get straight down to the business of learning. Our study suggests that it is not usually as straightforward as that.

In addition to the early orientation programmes that schools organise for new students, they also employ strategies that reinforce a sense of membership. In the next section we focus on these strategies — but we are also aware that the student body has its own system of membership. Where the formal, institutional concern is to help young people come to see themselves as members of a learning community, the memberships that the student group prize tend not to reflect the priority of academic learning. We move on from the discussion of membership to look at the ways in which labelling is used by teachers and by students to reinforce different versions of membership.

Membership

The school has a number of ways of developing a sense of 'institutional belonging'. For example, location maps of the school are often provided to help new students find their way round the buildings. There may be a Y7 notice board — 'That's good, that. It tells us what dinners and things we are on if we don't know'. There may be early induction activities where students have time off lessons to get to know members of their own form, and, later, competitions are organised across forms or houses that strengthen students' allegiance to their 'base' group; students are assigned a form tutor and a year (or house) tutor. The form tutor is a particularly important anchor for new students and it is helpful if she or he has an 'accepting' manner:

X (the form tutor) just like co-operates in our type of language. (Y8/M)

Like she knows which lessons we're doing and everything and she knows what it's like because she's quite young herself though, isn't she. It's not very long since she left school and she knows what it's like to be at school. (Y8/F)

While they are responding to the formal and informal procedures whereby the school helps them to feel comfortable, students are also having to learn the school's criteria for acceptance — its rules, the behaviours it values. As Ayers (1990: 272) has said, from the school's perspective the goal is to help students create 'an identity as industrious group members, develop a sense of belonging and of efficiency and productivity'. Ayers is here reminding us that institutional membership carries with it certain obligations.

In Y7 and Y8 most students are attempting to harmonise the conditions of membership offered by the school and its teachers and those offered by different groups of students. For instance, older students are providing encounters and events which mark the new students' entry into the student culture. The sense of advancement which is signified by the student being at secondary school is balanced both by students' awareness that they do not know the ropes and by the feeling of subordination (within the hierarchy) that the induction by older students seems designed to communicate. In our three schools peer induction included the usual rituals — being thrown over the wall or being thrown down the bank. The stories told in junior school were not entirely misleading! Indeed, Measor & Woods (1984: 27) argued that such myths are important because they signal the value of the informal student culture.

Membership, initially, is about security — both personal and interpersonal. Y8 students recalled a number of occasions when, as novice Y7s, they realised that they did not know their way around and were looking — and feeling — embarrassingly inept:

> It were half the form (went to the wrong room) and you're stood there with your white face saying, 'I'm sorry, I'm sorry'. You feel horrible. (Y8/F)

And the first disco:

> We ended up wearing jeans and a nice top and that and we wore high heels and everybody was like in trousers and shell suits and I just felt out of place. (Y8/F)

Or not knowing exactly what homework entails:

> Like I weren't really used to homework. I used to like not tell mum and dad about it and leave it in my bag and then I'd be doing it really late at night when I'm tired because like we didn't used to get any homework in junior school subjects then and I just didn't know what to do. (Y8/F)

At first, security resides in learning to be the same and do the same as everyone else. Yet schools have a commitment to ensuring that every student gains a sense of selfhood, and so strategies that focus individuality must also be introduced — such as certificates for effort: 'Not everyone has one', said one student, with pride.

The peer group offers different routes to security from those that teachers offer. Students may have the security of the friends who came with them from the same junior school, and in time many feel secure enough to find different or additional friends; there is security in finding out and following the fashions — whether it is a dress code in a school which has no official uniform, or, in one school, learning the rules of 'the chase' — a risky game which allows the more confident Y7 students to taunt older students and then to run away from them. Some Y7s misjudge their own capacity to survive at this one: 'Sometimes they get really scared. Like kids who are right small and can't run very fast'; and some find that they do not know the geography of the school well enough yet to know where to run to escape those in pursuit.

Certain kinds of membership, as well as the failure to achieve full institutional membership, can threaten academic learning. There are students who are 'off school' for a long time during the period of early socialisation through illness or accident and they can feel that they are behind with their work and don't know how to catch up. Moreover, the membership of their friendship group may change while they are away. There are also students who become apprehensive as a result of name calling or bullying and who stay away in order to avoid further harassment.

They are also at risk of falling behind in their work and losing their peer support group. A number of students recalled experiences in Y7 that made them reluctant to come to school. For example, this student:

> Like last year one of the fifth years came bullying me and I ended up with a black eye because he wopped me round the head with his bag... I didn't want to come to school because I was scared. (Y8/M)

Another talked about a girl, once a close friend, who rarely came to school:

> She's quite a good worker like but she's never here to learn. She used to be my best mate and then when she started not coming it got a bit hard because I had no one to sit with, so we're just good friends now because she never comes. (Y8/F)

Interestingly, with sustained support from her form and year tutor, the student made an effort in Y8 to attend regularly; she was helped by the readiness of her former friend to accept her back — she became a member of a group again rather than an odd isolate. But a boy in her form, also a regular non-attender by the end of Y7, was less fortunate. For a time he was a model of daring and style for the 'lads' in the group but as the dominance patterns among the regular attenders became established, so he became a threat to the leaders and was rejected. Towards the end of Y8 his occasional appearances were marked by more extreme disruptive behaviour and led not to admiration but to further rejection: at this time the school's efforts to reaffirm the need to learn in Y9 were beginning to be taken seriously and were having some impact even on the more unruly who had once been his mates: they now saw him as a threat to their capacity to start settling down and working harder. With no sense of 'belonging' in either the academic world of the school or the social life of his peers, the danger is that he will not re-establish himself as a student in this school.

There are also, of course, problems of students who are members of an anti-work group, some of whom may want to settle down and learn but who do not know how to, or do not dare to, become members of a more work-orientated group:

> I used to be on report cards, always getting done. It's kids in our form and that, and when you're with them you want to mess about like them so I had to talk to my form tutor. (Y8/M)

Another boy, who had been repeatedly on report, said that the only hope of changing his behaviour and having a chance to work was to join another form — but he knew that teachers and students in the 'receiving' form had 'learned' that students who changed forms were always troublemakers. His fear was that he would therefore be treated like a troublemaker in the new setting, even though he wanted to reform himself. He felt trapped and could see no easy way out.

The problems are not all to do with anti-work norms in friendship groups. In one Y8 form, three working class girls (two white and one black) have formed a friendship group. They see themselves as both different from and less able than their middle class peers: 'Everyone's brainy in our class apart from us... I would rather be in a class with all the thickheads'. They are aware that other students do not want to work with them: 'They always block us out like when we've got to work in groups; they always work and leave us'. And they describe what happened when two girls whom they regard as very posh were obliged to work with them:

> Yeah, and they were right 'orrible, saying, 'Oh, we don't want to work with yaw' (said in a mock middle class voice). They thought they'd 'ave to do all work an that 'cause they think we're right stupid.... (Y8/F)

Here a negative self-image is being reflected back to the three girls, largely on the basis of their being different in terms of class. They seem to cope by openly accepting the image — with a touch of bravado and amused self-mockery — and the close bonding that they feel for each other helps them to brush off the insults. However, the girls are also interpreting messages from some teachers as a reinforcement of their negative self identity: 'The teacher thinks we're right thick...' What we do not know is whether they are coming to believe the view of their ability that they perceive to be projected by both their peers and their teachers.

We also interviewed another group of three Asian girls, two of whom are confirmed in their friendship by the wariness of their peers who talk about sometimes 'ending up' having to work with them when the form is divided into small groups. (The third girl is considered 'okay' by her form classmates because she will talk to them in English.) Other students are suspicious of the two: 'They act like they don't understand English and (the teachers think they) never do anything (wrong). (But) they're just as bad as us at messing about an' all'. On one occasion, so another girl in their form claims, they called her — in English — 'some right swearing names' and when she retaliated, the teacher heard and she 'got done for it': the teacher had disbelieved her story — knowing that the Asian girls could speak little English. Thus, two of the Asian girls are beginning to be seen as devious as well as not very capable.

When students are ostracised for being different, whether through class or ethnicity, the support of friends is vital (Nilan, 1992) but we can see how easily other students — and sometimes teachers too — come to see the group that is different as academically weak; and how the members of the group may come, in time, to accept that definition of themselves.

Thus there is considerable diversity in the way that students explore what secondary school offers and decide what response to make. Within this diversity we identified a small number of students, across our three schools, who were clearly on the margins in terms of institutional membership and who, by the end of Year 8, were either not managing to be, or not wanting to be, re-integrated.

Labelling

Teachers as well as students use labelling as a means of defining membership and exclusion from membership. In both the teachers' and the students' systems, labels may refer directly to work and achievement, or they may refer to behaviour and personal characteristics that affect image and self image, and these may, in turn, affect work patterns. The effects of labelling can be positive or negative (Beynon, 1985).

Labelling takes many forms. The school is responsible for an early organisational form of labelling (which is essentially neutral) whereby students are known by their membership of a year group (e.g. Y7) or a form (e.g. Raleigh). These are shared labels. It also operates a more individualised labelling system through the process of giving praise and rewards to students whose academic — and sometimes non-academic — endeavours reflect the virtues that the school wishes to encourage. Thus the individual may come to be seen by teachers as 'bright', 'trying hard' and so on.

Some labels rest lightly while others are a source of embarrassment (for instance, the 'hard working' label that the teachers may value may be translated by the pupil culture into the negative label, 'boff'). The effects of being trapped in your own past behaviours, or in an image that is unfounded and reflects the bias of the observer, is disheartening and can be damaging (Hammersley & Woods, 1976). Certain kinds of report, as the students well know, stay in their file throughout the whole of their school career. A few students who had already been in a fair amount of trouble during their first year in secondary school were worried that the research interviews might somehow become part of the long-term baggage that they had to carry around with them: 'When we grow older will that be in a file or owt for when we get a job or owt like that?' What students do not seem to know — and this is perhaps disturbing in relation to those who see secondary school as a fresh start — is that they come with labels — the reports from their primary schools; they arrive at secondary school with pre-packaged reputations (Beynon, 1985; Metz, 1978). One of the concerns that emerged from this stage of the study was the difficulty students thought they had in struggling free from a negative image: they had not only to manage their own self-discipline but also to find a way of dissolving and reconstructing other people's expectations of them.

The school's use of rewards and reports as a way of shaping working habits will be looked at in the next section. Here we concentrate on the way that the student group uses labelling and the relationship between peer group labelling and learning.

The labels that students give each other reflect, on the whole, a fairly harsh system of norms and judgments. The mild end of the continuum is the use of nicknames. Nicknames can be good-humoured and accepting and they may be received with a degree of good humour — for example, a girl who gets called different brands of breakfast cereal:

> They used to call me Kellogg's Corn Flakes.
>
> Int: 'Why that?'
>
> Because my name's Rice — Rice Crispies. I get called Crispy and things like that. I didn't mind. I thought it were funny. (Y8/F)

But students are also sharp observers of who is different — for example, who is not wearing the right training shoes — and a less benign name-calling can follow. The quotation below refers to a girl who had become, by the second term of Y8, a fairly persistent non-attender but who was, in the third term, making a real effort to return — with the support of a friend, her form tutor and her year tutor. Her friend is talking:

> She told them (students who were harassing her) she was getting these trainers — Adidas Trojan — because people had been picking on her for her shoes and she told them she was getting them, but she weren't. She was saying that so they would be proud of her and everything... She has got quite a few problems at home.(Y8/F)

Another student was called names because of a skin disease which she tried hard to hide:

> She's small and she's got eczema, hasn't she, and a lot of people picked on her... People just pick on her like she's someat from outer space... Yes, I think that is why she does stop off (i.e. doesn't attend school). (Y8/F)

Once she confided in a few girls in her form, however, she was more protected:

> We weren't picking on her. We were just saying, 'God, what's wrong with you? and things, because we didn't know what was wrong with her — like she was keeping secrets from us. She was keeping things from us, like her eczema. She could have told us straight away. Now it seems like she trusts us more than the teachers. (Y8/F)

One boy who had been badly injured in an accident in Y7 is called names because, as he explained, he walks with a wobble. Another — a Y10 boy — has a severe speech defect; he is the victim of a particularly invidious form of harassment within the peer group culture — being called names by the younger students, including some from our Y8 form:

> We make fun out of his voice because he goes (imitates the sound). He's got no roof in his mouth. it's not his fault... He's used to it now... He knows it's a joke but he sometimes gets angry. (Y8/M)

This sharp marking of difference through name-calling can affect learning in a very direct way: it reduces self-confidence and students feel insecure within the peer group. It can lead to compensatory aggression — or it can lead students to opt out of school:

> It puts you off school (being called names). I didn't come to school a lot last year because they were calling me names. (Y8/M)

There is also a more subtle form of labelling through constant innuendo; the criticism is not explicitly voiced and the students who are on the receiving end come, in time, to hear most remarks as reinforcing the implied image of themselves. In one Y8 form there is a small group of girls who are looked down on by their peers — and also, they think, by some teachers. The girls talk here about how they are treated:

> I'm rubbish at everything.

> Miss Z thinks we're right thick...the teacher talks like extra slow as if we can't understand it or something.

We have been mainly talking about name-calling that attaches to particular individuals or groups, but there is also a generic name-calling that signifies an anti-work norm within the peer group. For instance, the word 'boff' is used to distance all those who are seen to be working hard or doing particularly well. Some students are strong enough to cope and their commitment to work is not affected by the name-calling, but others may find their loyalties divided — personally they want to do well but they also want to feel part of the group.

Students also trap each other — and themselves — in the labels they attach to forms. Part way through Y7, students develop a strong sense of membership of their own form (indeed in one form it became so strong that students who joined during the year felt excluded). They may start to label their form alongside others:

> Green's really bad. Yeah, because like half of them go round pinching stuff, people's pens, rulers and that. (Y8/M)

> Purple are all well behaved and everything. (Y8/M)

We do not yet know whether, and how, these form labels change as the students get older. They may be part of an early need, which the school endorses, to strengthen the students' sense of collective belonging. But as teaching in form groups gives way to teaching in cross-form groups or sets, so the instinct to label one's own group in relation to others may well fade; it remains to be seen whether it will be replaced by a labelling of groups by perceived ability. What is disturbing is that some forms within the year cohort come to be labelled quite early on as non-working, non-learning, and difficult to teach.

Enhancing the Status of Learning

From the beginning of Y7 secondary schools use various conventions to communicate the seriousness of learning. The most familiar — and universal — are homework, the regular reporting of individual progress and a system of incentives and rewards. In each sub-section we discuss in what ways the particular strategy manages to assign status to formal learning.

Homework

A homework policy assigns status to schoolwork through its power to invade out-of-school zones — which students may see as 'leisure' zones. The status is reinforced through the apparatus of homework books which are a reminder of the existence of a formal, daily homework schedule, and through the requirement that parents monitor the completion of homework and sign the homework book on a regular basis. The loophole in the system is that parents may not understand what proper completion of homework really means, and they may, in time, exercise their responsibility somewhat casually and even collude with students in signing the homework book when asked rather than when they are sure that the work has been done. How well does the system work?

The way in which homework tasks are set clearly relates to the way in which students respond to them; irregularity and inconsistency can quickly contribute to a loss of status in the eyes of students:

> They'll go about a month without giving you hardly any and then you'll get everything at once and you can't cope with it. (Y8/F)

> Sometimes in first year we didn't get any for weeks, but sometimes you get like three a night. (Y8/M)

This was a widespread reaction. Students were given homework timetables but teachers failed to make sure that they were adhered to. Not surprisingly, students then saw homework as less important than they had expected it to be. In one school, a student explained that teachers seemed to forget about homework after a while and then would suddenly all start giving it again — 'like they'd discussed it at the staff meeting' (Y8/F).

By the end of Year 7 many students were in the game of sussing out which teachers failed to collect in or check up on homework and this could mean that they would avoid doing it. They were also more confident in voicing concerns abut fairness and their rights. For instance, in Year 8, many students in one form were resisting doing homework in one subject because, in their eyes, it was not regarded as 'proper' homework but rather work which should have been done in the lesson had it been properly managed:

> Like...we get a whole side of A4 to do because he, our teacher, he's a really friendly man I suppose, but he talks all lesson...and then you have to write it all up at home. (Y8/F)

Students also suggested that teachers should be more aware of the demands they are under from other teachers — not realising that homework timetables are in fact an attempt to regulate the amount of homework set each evening and to protect students from overload:

> Some of the teachers don't realise how much homework you're getting from other teachers...if you do other things after school you don't often have the time, and when you have time you're either tired or you just don't want to do it and if you're not enjoying the topic anyway it doesn't really make you want to do it. (Y8/F)

Complaints such as this may, of course, reflect the view of homework that is held by many parents in communities where there is traditionally a sharp divide, particularly for men, between employment and leisure: in the workplace, what you do is determined by others whereas at home how time is spent is for the individual, not an 'authoritative other', to determine (see Harris et al., 1993). Overall, more boys than girls voiced strong opinions against homework. A typical argument was this: 'We have six hours to learn in school. That's enough' (Y8/M). In contrast, in one school, the importance of homework is generally reinforced by parents, as a teacher acknowledges: 'Parents want it and I give it. Most of them do it. It's that sort of school'.

Our data suggest that the effectiveness of homework policies in helping to establish the seriousness of learning is variable and is dependent on teachers working consistently to maintain the schedule of setting and responding to homework, or explaining why, on occasions, homework is not being set in a particular subject. It can also mean helping students and parents understand what kinds of things homework can achieve. 'I think it's really needed but I don't know why', said one student (Y8/M), while another saw homework as beneficial because his experience of being able to think quietly during the school day was negative: 'You'll take it home because, like, you can do it in silence and at school there's always talking' (Y8/M). It means ensuring that homework tasks are perceived by students as worthwhile and legitimate and not merely a 'left-over' from the lesson or a 'noddy' task that fulfils the demands of the schedule without contributing to real learning or to the consolidation of learning. Homework, if it is well managed, should advance learning and not contribute to its devaluing.

Incentives and rewards

Systems of incentives and rewards assign status to learning by selecting out and reinforcing certain forms of positive behaviour to do with commitment, perseverance, and success. The message is underlined in special events to honour, publicly, the achievement of those students who are judged to exemplify the virtues. Competition tends also to be an integral feature of incentives systems: students are encouraged to collect credits as a mark of individual recognition or as a means of helping their form to do well in the inter-form rivalries that help students to develop allegiance to a particular group and thereby strengthen their sense of institutional membership. They have something concrete to work for. However, for many students sporting achievement rather than academic learning tends to be the more powerful form of incentive through competition — at least at this stage of secondary schooling.

All three schools operate systems of incentives and rewards based on effort and achievement. However, the ways in which the systems are used by staff, even within the same school, may differ. Some staff place a great deal of importance on awarding merit marks or distributing credit stickers while others do not. Moreover, while many students recalled receiving a certificate or commendation as a 'good' moment for them, not all felt that such rewards were distributed fairly:

> ...some people try hard but they just don't do very well and teachers don't give them reward for that. I don't think that's particularly fair. (Y8/F)

As time goes on the reward system tends to lose some of its kudos. This may be because it becomes associated with a particular type of student: the boff who works consistently hard, does well and who, in some student cultures, is in the minority and likely to be a bit of an isolate. In time the system may lose status simply because it is not seen as 'cool', within a group-oriented student culture, for a minority of individuals to be singled out for recognition. It is at such a stage in students' school careers that teachers hope that learning is beginning to operate as an intrinsic reward system!

Progress in learning and progress reports

Individual progress reports assign status to learning in a distinctive way. They begin to build a sense of the continuity of a student's learning and are a means of emphasising individual responsibility and accountability. There may be some ambiguity in the fact that reports deal also with behavioural issues; clearly, patterns of attendance and classroom concentration affect learning in direct ways but it can easily happen that students and their parents or guardians respond more strongly to messages about 'discipline', which are easy to understand, than to messages about learning, which are perhaps more complex and subtle.

In all three schools students receive regular progress reports although the format varies; the end of year report is invariably the fullest. Such reports can help students to understand how teachers are perceiving them as individuals. For researchers, reports are a useful means of comparing students' perceptions of how they are getting on at school with their teachers' perceptions.

The individual report may not always communicate effectively in Y7 and Y8. For instance, the self-image that a report offers is constructed out of a teacher vocabulary that can sound out-of-tune with the students' own vocabulary. Here, a student is struggling to take on board how a teacher has described him; he tries to give meaning to the teacher's words through a concrete example:

> I had a poor attitude towards my lessons. I ain't got no self control either. Like if I see dices I'll pick them up and start playing with them. And my writing's always messy and my spelling's atrocious. (Y8/M)

This is a student who wants to do better and who accepts the criticism as a guide to improvement. Sometimes, however, a student may misread a teacher's comments. For instance, teachers are usually trying hard to be encouraging in the early reports. They, of course, understand the subtle inflections and wordings that signal their concern — but students are not yet attuned and may only 'hear' if criticism is unambiguously sharp. For example:

> In my report the teachers haven't said any comments that sound worrying to me and he's (year/house tutor) just said 'this is very worrying' or something like that. I thought it were a good report because I didn't have any bad comments on it. (Y8/M)

In some cases the root of the misinterpretation seems to be that the student does not understand the responsibility of the year/house tutor to construct an overall comment out of the totality of individual teachers' remarks. This responsibility can seem strange to a student if she or he does not really know — i.e. is not taught by — the year/house tutor and the report may be rejected because the overall comment seems, on the face of it, to be invalid or 'unfair'; the student may not feel that the year/house tutor is in a position to comment:

> Mine said, 'This child's report is really worrying' and (the tutor) doesn't even know us or seen us work or anything. (Y8/M)

Perhaps the greatest challenge for secondary schools is to ensure that progress in learning in Year 7 — after the high, if nervous expectations that students often have at the point of transition — does not stand still or even go backwards. The problem is compounded at the moment by the national preoccupation with parental choice which means that secondary schools are likely to recruit from a larger number of primary schools. The result is that teachers may have to deal with tremendous diversity, within their Year 7 groups, of content knowledge and teaching-learning styles. Clearly the National Curriculum is designed to remove the content dimension of this problem. In 1991, however, when we were starting our fieldwork, the problem was still there and for some students their early experiences of learning in secondary school were stressful and were leading to a lowering of self-esteem:

> It's right hard, French, because we hadn't done it... They can all talk French and we can't do it. I'm right rubbish... That's why teacher thinks we're stupid or something. I hate French... So we are going ask her to move today. We just don't like it; it's too hard. Because they have been doing it for about a million years. (Y8/F)

When it comes to repetition of work already done there were some students who were in danger of losing interest in some subjects but there were others who started secondary school feeling nervous about their capacity to keep up and they accepted — even welcomed — going over familiar ground. It gave them a sense of security; it served to reinforce what they already knew and gave them more time to settle in slowly and adjust to the new demands.

Marking Students' Passage through Secondary School

By the end of Y8 most students felt that they had been accepted both by the peer group and by teachers, but there were some who did not feel totally comfortable with the ways of the school, who knew that they did not have friends they could rely on, or who did not feel totally at ease with themselves as learners. We have identified some of the reasons why this is so: some students miss school because of illness, anxiety or other reasons and may fall behind and feel academically disoriented or socially lost; others — especially those for whom puberty comes early — are finding that academic concerns are less preoccupying than the excitements of their social and sexual adventuring; some may find themselves caught up with groups of young people outside school that have their own dynamic and that are very difficult to break away from.

There are also other students whose early profile seems more settled but who, during Year 8, when the initial upheavals of transition have given way to a more predictable regularity, can become restless: 'You think, "Oh God. I've got this today" and so on and you don't feel excited any more coming to school'. Others are feeling more adult — in terms of simply being older and taller and also because they are not now the youngest in the school — and are beginning to seek greater autonomy in their learning. These students also need to 'see' and encounter new challenges in their Y8 work. As one student said of her friend: 'Jennifer's not intellectually stimulated yet' (Y8/F).

By Y8 students were generally beginning to think about the balance of 'fun' and 'serious work' and to think about their own work patterns; some were also beginning to try out their own individuality in relation to the pressures and loyalties of membership of their form or class. The following quotations give some sense of the way that these pupils are beginning to reflect on the way they use their time in school and the way they relate to their peers:

> I don't like mess about right badly but have a bit of a laugh. You can't sit there and work *all* lesson. (Y8/F)

> If I work too much I just lose my concentration and mess about anyway so I might as well mess about first and then get down to some work. (Y8/F)

We did find evidence of gendered perspectives here, with boys more inclined to talk in a laid back way about learning and futures; a minority had worked out, by Y8, that it was possible to calculate the minimum needed to get by and then work harder when it became really necessary:

> What's the point? At the moment I don't get anything from it. At GCSE I do, but in the second year, no. (Y8/M)

The trend towards less course-work at Key Stage 4 and a higher profile for the examination itself offers support for such a strategy, of course.

Y7 has its own distinctive character and challenges — getting used to the new teachers, the students, the regime, and so on. Our interview data highlight the compelling and confusing experiences, the anxiety and the excitement of the first couple of terms. Looking back, the students realise that Y7 is different: 'Y7s get treated really nicely'. They then see Y9 as offering a new set of challenges. This is the year when the learning really begins to get tough: all our schools introduced setting in at least one subject in Y9; the students also knew that SATs and options lay ahead. The knowledge that such things await them engenders a mixture of anxiety and excitement that seems capable of competing with some of the external and social rivals for students' attention. Y8, in contrast, has no such visible features: it presents a relatively flat terrain. It is, however, the year when students discover that they actually have some responsibility for their own learning, and they vary in their responses to this awareness.

The task for the schools seems to be to prevent Y8 from being experienced as a relatively 'fallow' year in terms of academic learning. Schools may need to find more ways of 'staging' the novelties of secondary schooling — not in any sense to trivialise schooling but instead to mark the importance of the opportunities for learning and the seriousness of the challenges. At the same time, such staging, or 'marking', might also reflect the growth in the students' sense of adult self that most are beginning to acknowledge during Y8.

Notes

1. A shorter and slightly differently focused version of this paper has appeared in the *British Journal of Educational Psychology* (1993), 63, 322–336.
2. In September 1992 we lost Dr David Gillborn but he was replaced by Dr Gwen Wallace, who has taken over the fieldwork in the school he was working in.

References

Ayers, W. (1990) Small heroes: In and out of school with 10 year old city kids. *Cambridge Journal of Education* 20 (3), 269–76.
Beynon, J. (1985) *Initial Encounters in the Secondary School*. Lewes: Falmer Press.
Cullingford, C. (1991) *The Inner World of the School*. London: Cassell.
Furlong, V. J. (1976) Interaction sets in the classroom: Towards a study of pupil knowledge. In M. Hammersley and P. Woods (eds) *The Process of Schooling*. London: Routledge and Kegan Paul.
Goffman, E. (1961) *Asylums: Essays on the Social Situation of Mental Patients and Other Inmates*. Harmondsworth: Penguin.
Hammersley, M. and Woods, P. (eds) (1976) *The Process of Schooling*. London: Routledge and Kegan Paul.
Harris, S., Nixon, J. and Rudduck, J. (1993) School work, homework and gender. *Gender and Education* 5 (1), 3–15.
Measor, L. and Woods, P. (1984) *Changing Schools*. Milton Keynes: Open University Press.
Metz, M.H. (1978) *Classrooms and Corridors: The Crisis of Authority in Desegregated Secondary Schools*. Berkeley: University of California Press.
Nilan, D. (1992) Kazzies, DBTs and Tryhards: Categories of style in adolescent girls' talk. *British Journal of Sociology of Education* 13 (2), 201–14.

Pollard, A. (1985) *The Social World of the Primary School.* London: Holt, Rinehart and Winston.

Waterhouse, S. (1992) *First Episodes: Pupil Careers in the Early Years of School.* Lewes: Falmer Press.

Woods, P. (1980) *Pupil Strategies.* London: Croom Helm.

— (1981) Strategies, commitment and identity. In L. Barton and S. Walker (eds) *Schools, Teachers and Teaching.* Lewes: Falmer Press.

5 Perceptions of Language and Language Learning in English and Foreign Language Classrooms

ROSAMOND MITCHELL, CHRISTOPHER BRUMFIT
and JANET HOOPER

Introduction

For many years the contribution of metalinguistic understanding (and especially, the study of grammar) to language learning and language development has been a contentious issue. Traditionally, the study of grammar was at the core of language education (Howatt, 1984). In recent decades, however, in the teaching of both English and foreign languages, experiential models of learning have come to dominate, and explicit discussion and analysis of language has been marginalised as unlikely to make any significant contribution to language development. (For typical examples of this line of argument, see e.g. Allen, 1988 for English as a mother tongue and Krashen, 1981 for foreign languages.)

Currently, however, there is a revival of interest in 'knowledge about language' as a valid element in the broader language curriculum; this can be seen plainly in the institution of a 'knowledge about language' (KAL) element in the National Curriculum for English (DES, 1990), building on the earlier work of the Kingman Committee (DES, 1988). Ambiguities remain, however, concerning possible rationales for this revival. Outside professional educational circles, strong beliefs persist that English language standards are declining, and that the best way of combating this decline is a return to traditional explicit grammar teaching in schools. Press reactions to the Cox Report (DES, 1989), for example, strongly supported this view — though the 'language complaint' tradition has a long pedigree, as Milroy & Milroy (1985) demonstrate.

The so-called 'Language Awareness' movement of the 1980s has promoted alternative rationales in addition (Donmall, 1985). Firstly, the view has been taken (particularly by foreign language teachers) that motivation for language learning can be significantly improved by the study of topics such as relationships between different languages, and language development in young children. Secondly, it has been argued that the study of language is essential to an understanding of the human condition, through awareness of the nature of social interaction, and of personal identity expressed through language choice (Language Awareness Working Party, 1985). It has similarly been argued that an explicit study of individual and societal bi- and multilingualism is a core element in a multicultural curriculum for all pupils (DES, 1985; Houlton, 1985). English teachers have likewise been familiarised with aspects of language variation such as accent, dialect, audience or style by leading figures such as James Britton and Harold Rosen, and encouraged to promote conscious understanding of such aspects among pupils, from similar motives to those of the language awareness movement (see e.g. Allen, 1988).

This complex debate has however been underpinned by very little empirical research into how language is viewed by ordinary teachers and pupils, how it is actually talked about in language classrooms, and what kinds of 'models' and understandings of the nature of language are developed by pupils as a result. The large volume of classroom language research conducted in recent years has concerned itself with language as communication, as social interaction, and as means of cognitive and/or affective growth, as well as means of control (Edwards & Westgate, 1987), but has paid little attention to metalinguistic dimensions. There has been only limited exploration of the models of language available even to teachers (e.g. Chandler, 1988; Mitchell & Hooper, 1992), and isolated commentary on the nature of classroom talk about language, for example Faerch (1985, 1986) on foreign languages.

We are currently (1991–93) conducting a study designed first of all to investigate how language gets talked about in contemporary English and foreign language classrooms. In addition, the project is exploring the models of language available to both teachers and pupils, and their perceptions regarding the contribution of 'knowledge about language' (KAL) to language development. The study focuses on secondary schools, where pupils are in contact with a range of language professionals with potentially conflicting 'models' of language, and where they may also be expected to be developing relatively elaborated and stable levels of understanding, partly via 'folk' linguistics absorbed outside the classroom, and partly from classroom experience.

The aims of the project are primarily descriptive, and the methodology is that of case study, combining qualitative and quantitative methods of data analysis. During 1991/92, Year 9 pupils in three Hampshire secondary schools have been observed and audiorecorded through extended (8 week) parallel sequences of English and foreign languages lessons (covering French, German and Spanish); in addition, they have participated in a variety of special tasks and interviews designed to explore their understandings of the nature of language, including commentaries and discussions on classwork, both oral and written. Their teachers have participated in a variety of interviews covering their theories of language development, rationales for their classroom practices, and their beliefs about the place of knowledge about language in language education. They have also been asked to comment systematically on the possible contribution of 'knowledge about language' (KAL) to specific pieces of pupils' work, oral and written, produced in the normal course of classroom activity.

This chapter presents preliminary findings on contrasting models of language, and theories of language development, prevailing in the contemporary practice of the English and foreign languages classroom. The procedures which have been developed within the project to explore participants' models of language, including their beliefs regarding the relationship between 'knowledge about language' and language development, are also briefly outlined.

Preliminary Findings: Models of Language in the Classroom

The fieldwork phase of the research has only just been completed (summer 1992); consequently, no detailed analysis of the observational data has as yet been completed, though preliminary analyses have been undertaken. The account below provides a brief and impressionistic account of the handling of language in two of the case-study schools only, based on our classroom observations, taking each subject area separately. In these schools at least, it seemed that broadly similar trends were revealed within each subject area, while English and foreign languages produced quite strongly contrasting cross-subject profiles.

The foreign languages classroom

In the foreign languages (FLs) classrooms, topic areas (such as ordering meals in French restaurants, going to the doctors) were the main organising constructs perceived by pupils. However, units of work with an overt topical focus typically served as vehicles for substantial structural content (morphology and/or syntax), in the coursebooks generally followed.

Whether teaching this material inductively or deductively, the FLs teachers generally seemed to adhere to a 'bottom-up' language learning theory, with an emphasis on the recognition and acquisition of discrete vocabulary items, and the subsequent construction of spoken and written sentences. Consequently, language was dealt with largely at word and sentence level, and texts of any substantial length were rarely in evidence in FLs classrooms. When longer texts *were* a focus for listening or reading, there was a tendency for the teachers to break them down into smaller units. The exception to this was in the classroom where the teacher used the target language most consistently as a medium of communication; here, longer stretches of classroom discourse occurred to an extent naturally, when, for example, the teacher was talking to pupils about particular features of the target culture.

Despite following a similar, largely structural pedagogic framework, the different FLs teachers observed varied considerably in the degree of explicit attention paid to KAL topics. The teacher who handled the structural framework with the least amount of explicit comment was also the one already mentioned as the most consistent user of the target language as a medium of classroom communication. However, her lessons too encompassed some brief KAL-focused episodes, in which features of the grammatical system were highlighted (in the target language) and pupils were asked to derive the 'rule' from having seen it in use, perhaps write brief grammar notes (in English), and then move sometimes into a practice phase, in the form of a short oral or written exercise.

The remaining FLs teachers observed in these two schools paid substantial overt attention to grammar, with systematic exposition in English of French morphology in one classroom, and of basic sentence patterns in another. In both these classrooms such pre-planned KAL episodes took place regularly, and in addition one teacher regularly suggested a variety of analytic strategies more responsively, as pupils encountered unfamiliar vocabulary.

The main KAL focus in these FLs lessons thus concerned areas of morphology and syntax; the only substantial additional focus was the attention paid in one classroom to learning strategies, where the teacher regularly concluded her lessons with an invitation to reflect (in English) on what had been learned that day, and how, these discussions largely centring on strategies for the memorisation and recall of discrete vocabulary items.

The English classroom

In stark contrast with the FLs classes, talk about language in the English lessons was broadly concerned with function rather than with form, and was very firmly centred around texts, rather than words or sentences. In both schools it was made clear from the outset; in the initial teacher interviews, that 'knowledge about language' work was meant to arise, as a matter of policy, out of and alongside the work pupils were doing. Both English Heads of Department also said, however, that the National Curriculum proposals in this area had made them look more closely at how they were already dealing with knowledge about language; as a consequence, their departments were tending to make such work more systematic and more explicit.

In one school, for example, the English Department was in the process of incorporating a KAL module into its schemes of work for each year, with a planned module for Year 9 on 'repertoires of language'. It was clear, however, from the classroom observation, that language work was at present still largely arising out of the thematic text-based units of work that provided the broad structure within which the English teacher operated.

Twelve of the fifteen English lessons seen in this school centred around a Shakespeare text. The talk about language that arose across and out of these lessons was concerned variously with the contrast between 'old' and 'modern' language, the differing styles and language of newspaper reporting, and feedback on performed readings. However, such talk tended to be of a somewhat intermittent nature, and it seemed that for the pupils actively to engage with a task took clear priority over the reflective activity that might precede or follow. Most striking in this respect was the time devoted to readings of scenes from the text; over the three lessons recorded of this type, little talk *about* the activity was in evidence, either from the pupils in their groups or from the teacher as she heard them engage, very enthusiastically for the most part, with the text. Indeed, the only episodes of any length involving explicit talk about language in this particular unit occurred in response to a batch of written work where the control of punctuation was deemed poor enough to warrant special attention.

In the subsequent unit, by contrast, there was a good deal of (planned) talk about language. The class was moving into a unit of work on poetry, and here — as indeed in the other English classroom — the willingness of the teacher to use technical terms in the *literary* area was striking. Where it was rare for a teacher or pupil in the English lessons to refer to language in morpho-syntactic terms, it was common for quite sophisticated meta-linguistic terms to be used in the area of literature: *simile, metaphor, alliteration* and *imagery*, for example.

In the second school, ten of the twenty-six English lessons observed were taken up with study of a particular narrative text, through which the teacher was pursuing a number of concurrent aims. Talk about language was most readily discernible through an intermittently overt focus on the language of story-telling, which was an underlying planned concern that only surfaced *explicitly* from time to time, partly in the service of the conscious crafting of a piece of descriptive writing towards which the pupils were being directed by the teacher. Such explicit talk was typically interwoven with discussion of the broader themes of the novel itself and their interrelation with the real-life concerns of the pupils, to which the teacher frequently appealed in eliciting memories, feelings and personal anecdotes. In the introductory lesson, then, the teacher announced that they were embarking on a literature study, and spent a substantial part of the session exploring different genres of 'storying' with the pupils, partly through appealing to the knowledge and associations they brought with them, partly via use of the thesaurus, before moving in from the broader consideration of the language of story-telling to the specific focus of the chosen novel, based around legend and superstition. Some lessons later, the concern with the crafting of a story surfaced more explicitly again, as the teacher encouraged the pupils to recapture the details of a personal encounter with a 'strange' person through anecdote and through a 'word-blast', jotting down keywords and phrases to bring that person back to life. In a subsequent lesson, they were given the homework task of shaping these initial thoughts into a draft plan of the description of a meeting with a stranger or recluse.

Such *explicit* KAL episodes were always set alongside the reading of the novel itself, and the ongoing discussion of its themes and their relation to the real world, in terms of both the pupils' personal experiences and the wider human concerns spiralling out from those; there was thus a continuing sense of continuity, that the text study and the move towards a piece of descriptive writing were simultaneously leading into and out of the pupils' own concerns and experiences. The teacher drew also on a variety of literary and cultural sources; in a later lesson, for example, an extract from a Dickens story, linked thematically to the class novel, also became the focus for a further explicit consideration of the crafting of a piece of descriptive writing.

Talk About Language: Preliminary Conclusions

As the project proceeds, the rich data base of lesson notes and recordings gathered during 1991/92 will be analysed much more systematically, and interpretations tentatively suggested here will be more thoroughly tested and developed. However, the brief examples given above already suggest that substantial differences continue to exist in the range of KAL topics dealt with, and the ways in which they are handled, in English and FLs classrooms. (This is true though neither as yet shows particular conformity with National Curriculum thinking on KAL.)

The FLs examples cited indicate substantial teacher commitment to explicit KAL-related talk, but with a fairly narrow and traditional focus on matters of syntax and, especially, morphology. This system focus at a fairly micro level in turn seems linked to the nature of the coursebook syllabuses being followed, to a preoccupation with smaller rather than larger text units, and to the 'bottom up' language learning theories which may be read into classroom instructional patterns.

In the English classrooms visited, by contrast, explicit attention to matters of syntactic form is rare and unsystematic, except as evidenced in responsive written comments on individual pieces of work returned to pupils, where errors of punctuation, spelling or syntax are an occasional focus. Explicit talk about language in these classrooms is much more likely to have an orientation to function, appropriacy, or especially to literary style, than to 'language system' issues; and the explicit KAL episodes observed arise most commonly in the course of study of much more substantial texts, such as plays, poems and novels. Again, explanations for this apparent pattern are to be sought both in teachers' subject ideologies, and in their theories of language development, as our work progresses.

Clearly, it is too early for any statement to be made about the initial differences perceived. Closer inspection of the data base may lead us to modify our positions substantially, to detect greater similarities or other differences. However, it is evident that subject-based differences of perception about the nature and relevance of KAL may be significant for the overall picture of language that learners obtain in secondary school.

Exploring Participants' Knowledge About Language

The teachers

The English and foreign languages teachers collaborating in the project have been interviewed at a number of points during the fieldwork phase. Preliminary interviews conducted prior to the observational phase, in summer/autumn 1991, explored their reported teaching strategies relating to language, their beliefs about the nature of language and language learning, and the possible contribution made to language development by systematic metalinguistic discussion and analysis. In this interview, teachers' reactions to the National Curriculum and its proposals for 'knowledge about language' were also explored. During the course of the lesson observations during 1991/2, continuing informal discussions were held with the teachers, primarily to monitor the decision-making underlying the teaching strategies observed, and especially teachers' rationales for promoting particular types of KAL-related discussion. Further interviews took place at the end of the extended period of observation with each individual, and subsequently at the end of the year (i.e. in summer 1992). These post-observation interviews probed teachers' impressions of the progress made by the classes observed, and major influences on that progress; they also allowed the researchers to explore teachers' reactions to evolving National Curriculum policy for languages, and their developing strategies for implementing appropriate Programmes of Study, especially in the KAL area.

In the course of an extended final interview, the teachers were also asked to comment in detail on specific pieces of work produced by selected Year 9 pupils, either in class or as normal homework. These pieces of work included poems, book reviews and essays (in English), sentence-length exercises, letters and oral role plays (in foreign languages). In each case, the teachers were asked to explain their own goals in setting the task, the guidance given, and the sources of advice/input they would expect pupils to use in carrying out the task. They were then asked to evaluate the individual pieces of work, commenting on the extent to which advice given had been followed, and providing a rationale for the kind of feedback which had been/would be provided for the pupils concerned. It is hoped that these commentaries (not yet analysed) will yield fuller insights into the teachers' beliefs about the role of metalinguistic analysis and discussion in improving aspects of language performance, oral or written.

The pupils

While classroom observation reveals much about teachers' models of language, theories of language development, and beliefs about the place of KAL in language education, it inevitably reveals much less about the beliefs and understandings of the pupils. Special complementary efforts have therefore been made throughout the periods of lesson observations, and also in a final phase of special activities conducted in the summer of 1992, to explore pupils' knowledge and beliefs through a variety of tasks conducted outside 'normal' language lessons. These activities have aimed to explore pupils' own understandings of the nature of language, the origins of pupils' KAL, and their beliefs about the relationship of such knowledge with language development.

Firstly, during the later stages of the 8-week periods of lesson observation and recording with each class, a variety of opportunities were taken to extract pupils from lessons in small friendship groups. In these small group sessions, the pupils were asked to comment on selected activities seen in class, or to comment on aspects of their own performance (written or spoken), and on the feedback they had received. These discussions sought to clarify pupils' perception of aspects of knowledge about language currently being focused on by the teacher. For example, after a foreign language lesson, pupils might be asked to explain the grammatical structure being practised (e.g. gender agreement in French); after an English activity in which pairs of pupils had been videoed interviewing each other on their reading preferences, pupils were asked about the qualities of successful interviews.

These early discussions with pupils had the advantages, and the limitations, of highly contextualised focus. On the one hand, detailed analysis of this material should yield us useful insights into what pupils were making of KAL topics currently being consciously focused on by their teachers; on the other hand, such local discussions cannot be relied on to provide any kind of general overview of the state of pupils' 'knowledge about language' overall.

On the conclusion of the observational phase, therefore, at Easter 1992, a final phase was begun, which took a more systematic approach to the exploration of pupils' knowledge about language. Arising out of our reading of current discussions of KAL (e.g. the Kingman Report (DES, 1988) or the unpublished materials produced by the Language in the National Curriculum — LINC — project), as well as out of our own classroom observations, we had produced a checklist of five dimensions of knowledge about language on which classroom discussions might be expected to centre. These were:

(1) Language as system.
(2) Language acquisition.
(3) Language change through time.
(4) Styles and genres of language.
(5) Social and regional variation.

For each of these KAL areas, it was decided to produce a variety of activities which could be undertaken by pairs or small groups of pupils, which were designed to explore pupils' knowledge and beliefs within the area. The tasks typically provided a stimulus, often in the form of some kind of language data, plus a range of discussion questions and/or simple analyses to be undertaken with the data. It was planned that some tasks would be guided by the participation of a member of the research team, but that others could be undertaken by groups of pupils without adult involvement. A number of light, cheap sets of recording equipment were assembled, so that an entire class could if necessary be recorded at one time, undertaking the tasks in a number of small groups, each working at their own pace.

During the spring of 1992, a large variety of tasks were trialled by members of the research team, with Year 9 classes in several schools other than the main case study schools. The trialling process led to a fairly ruthless weeding out of tasks, but a final set of 13 tasks (between one and four per KAL area) was judged sufficiently productive for use in the case study schools. Thus for example, in the 'Language as System' area, four tasks were used (see Appendix for examples of tasks 1c and 1d). The first task, called 'Jumbled Words', provided pupils with a mix of real English function words, and nonsense content words, printed individually on bits of card. Pupils were asked to create sentences using this material, and to make up a meaning for their 'sentence', commenting on their reasoning as they did so. Obviously, this task was intended to explore pupils' awareness of morphology and grammatical categories. A second task, 'Jumbled Sentences', provided pupils with complete texts (narrative and non-narrative), dismembered into their component sentences. Again, the task was to reconstruct the text, and to explain the reasoning behind the sequencing proposed; the aim was to elicit pupils' awareness of textual structure above the level of the sentence, and capacity to talk about it. A third task, 'Toddler's Talk' (1c), provided sample utterances produced by a two year old child, and asked pupils to identify patterns in the 'errors' made by the child; the fourth, 'Wang Min's and Paolo's Mistakes' (1d), was similar, but used utterances produced by learners of English as a foreign language.

The researchers' hope was that relatively free discussion by the pupils of such material would provide evidence not only of pupils' practical linguistic competence (as shown in the successful solution of the various puzzles presented by the tasks), but more importantly, of their understanding of how language operates as a system, and their capacity to make explicit the constructs and categories on which they were drawing in completing the tasks. In the event, some of the tasks required a continuing researcher presence, to elicit the reasoning underlying practical decision-making (e.g. the 'Jumbled Words' task); others elicited data relevant not only for the area with which the task was associated, but for others too. (So, 'Toddler's Talk' has elicited some material relevant for the 'Language Acquisition' area, as might have been expected.) The resulting large corpus of data has not yet begun to be systematically analysed; we are optimistic that meaningful patterns will emerge, though all the pointers so far suggest that Year 9 pupils' KAL is neither very systematic nor very elaborated.

The last major elicitation procedure used with pupils parallels that used with their teachers. Six pupils in each class, drawn in pairs at random from those identified by their teacher as belonging in high, mid and low ability bands, were asked to comment on a piece of classwork or homework they had recently produced, normally written work. (This was the only occasion when pupils were interviewed individually.) They were asked to explain the guidance they had been given for the work; the sources of advice and help they had used in carrying it out; their own evaluation of the work; and their perceptions of teacher feedback on it, if any. Once again, these comments will be analysed, to explore the perceived role of metalinguistic discussion, in planning and carrying out language work, and in making changes and improvements.

Conclusion

This chapter has been very much an account of work in progress. We anticipate that once completed, the work will fill a gap in providing an account of contemporary practice in a contested area, and contribute useful evidence to continuing debates on the proper place for KAL in different types of language classroom. At this mid point, we would very much welcome comments especially on our methodology, and are interested in contacting others interested in the promotion of a reflective pedagogy, and exploring the constructive role of metastatement, within and beyond the language classroom.

References

Allen, D. (1988) *English, Whose English?* Sheffield: NATE, for NAAE.

Chandler, R. (1988) Unproductive busywork. *English in Education* 22 (3), 20–8.

DES (1985) *Education for All* (Swann Report). London: HMSO.

— (1988) *Report of the Committee of Inquiry into the Teaching of English Language* (Kingman Report). London: HMSO.

— (1989) *English for Ages 5 to 16* (Cox Report). London: HMSO.

— (1990) *English in the National Curriculum (No 2)*. London: HMSO.

Donmall, B.G. (ed.) (1985) *Language Awareness* (NCLE Papers and Reports 6). London: CILT.

Edwards, A.D, and Westgate, D.P.G. (1987) *Investigating Classroom Talk*. Lewes: Falmer.

Faerch, C. (1985) Meta talk in FL classroom discourse. *Studies in Second Language Acquisition* 7, 184–99.

— (1986) Rules of thumb and other teacher-formulated rules in the foreign language classroom. In G. Kasper (ed.) *Language, Teaching and Communication in the Foreign Language Classroom* (pp. 125–43). Aarhus: Aarhus University Press.

Houlton, D. (1985) *All Our Languages*. London: Edward Arnold.

Howatt, A.P.R. (1984) *A History of English Language Teaching*. Oxford: Oxford University Press.

Krashen, S.D. (1981) *Second Language Acquisition and Second Language Learning*. Oxford: Pergamon.

Language Awareness Working Party (1985) The Report. In B.G. Donmall (ed.), pp. 1–30.

Milroy, J., and Milroy, L. (1985) *Authority in Language*. London: Routledge.
Mitchell, R., and Hooper, J. (1992) Teachers' views on language knowledge. In C. James and P. Garrett (eds) *Language Awareness in the Classroom* (pp. 40–50). Harlow: Longman.

Appendix

Task 1c: Toddlers' talk

Instructions to pupils

You are doing a group project on how toddlers learn language and you have managed to collect together a number of examples of how a typical two-year-old speaks [see the attached sheet].

Your list contains several examples of things little Ben has said over the past few weeks.

Read through each example together, and discuss what mistakes Ben has made in the way he says things.

(1) Pick out the mistakes and correct each one: how would *you* have said it?

(2) When you have been through all the examples, look back and discuss what sorts of things he gets wrong: are there any mistakes he *often* makes?

(3) Which do you think are his *two* most important types of mistake? Say what sorts of mistakes they are, and give an example of each one.

These are some of the things two-year-old Ben has said :

[N.B. The bits in brackets tell you more about what is happening at the time Ben is speaking.]

(1) Want Ben go in garden, Mummy!

(2) Look, Mummy! Ben have dinner. [Ben's eating some beans on toast.]

(3) Daddy no go out, Daddy read story. [Ben doesn't want his Daddy to go out.]

(4) Look, Daddy! Ben done wee-wee on carpet!

(5) No Mummy eat grapes. Mine!

(6) Ben go out last night, see that big train.

(7) Ben little bit frightened, that train noisy.

(8) That baby cry, Mummy.

(9) Want Ben see train.

(10) Ben no must open that. [Ben has a bottle of nail-polish.]

Task 1d: Wang Min's and Paolo's mistakes

Instructions to Pupils

Wang Min is Chinese and Paolo is Spanish: they are foreign students who are learning English. Here are two extracts from conversations they each had with Claire, who is English.

Read through the conversation extracts, and pick out all the mistakes that Wang Min and Paolo make with their English.

In your group, talk about each mistake:

(a) What would it be in correct English?
(b) Why did Wang Min and Paolo make those mistakes?

In your group, discuss how you would explain to the foreign students what it is that they're doing wrong. Do they make the same sort of mistake more than once?

(c) Now pick out one or two mistakes in each extract, and write them down. Next to each one, write a sentence explaining to Wang Min or Paolo *why* it is not correct English.

Extract A

Wang Min:	She think my English better, she say it good. I am surprised — I think my English worse, not good.
Claire:	It's good. It's improved a lot. Are you still going to your lessons?
Wang Min:	Yes, and talk to other teacher.
Claire:	So you still go to the Language Centre?
Wang Min:	In the last year I went to Language Centre. This year, I no go to Language Centre.

Extract B

Claire:	How does the education system in Spain work then?
Paolo:	Is like the English education, because we go to the school when we are three years old.
Claire:	Three? That's young.
Paolo:	And then when they are six years old they start the general education to the fourteen.
Claire:	Mm hm.
Paolo:	And then when anybody finish the general education he take the exams — is like... I don't know what is it called in England.

6 Teachers' and Pupils' Perceptions of Effective Classroom Learning: Conflicts and Commonalities

PAUL COOPER and DONALD McINTYRE

Introduction

This chapter reports preliminary findings of a study of teachers' and Year 7 pupils' perceptions of effective classroom learning in English and history. The findings, which bear the status of *tentative hypotheses*, are based on an initial analysis of the data. More complete and detailed findings will be presented at a later date. The particular focus of this chapter is the extent and nature of commonality between teacher and pupil perceptions.

The present study is based on the idea that experienced teachers are in possession of extensive and complex 'craft knowledge' which enables them to engage in effective teaching in classrooms, at least some of the time. More tentatively, we are concerned with the possibility that pupils too have their own brand of craft knowledge, which they use in the learning process. The theory of craft knowledge that underpins the project is derived from work by Desforges & McNamara (1977, 1979), and Brown & McIntyre (1993). The criteria for what is meant by 'effective' is part of teachers' and pupils' craft knowledge, as is the knowledge of means by which such effectiveness is achieved. The intention of the research is to access and describe this knowledge, and to explore the ways in which teachers' and pupils' perceptions can be related one to the other. Within the general concern with craft knowledge a particular focus of the research is on subject teaching and learning, and teachers' ways of construing and taking account of individual differences among pupils. The research is taking place within the context of the newly introduced National Curriculum in English and history (in England and Wales), therefore teachers' responses to this and its perceived effects on their thinking and practice provide an additional focus.

Sample and Method

Eight English teachers, five history teachers, and their respective Year 7 classes were the subjects of the study. These were studied over three four hour (approximately) units of lessons throughout the academic year 1991–92. The aim of the research is to enable teachers and pupils to articulate their authentic understandings of effective classroom learning. The method chosen to achieve this was 'informant' style interviewing (Powney & Watts, 1987) combined with participant observation. After observing particular lessons, the researcher conducted separate interviews with teachers and a sample of pupils. In these interviews teachers and pupils were asked to talk about their experience of the events of the lesson, and to talk in particular about things that they believe went well in the lesson, from a teaching and learning point of view. The interviews then proceeded with the interviewer seeking exemplification and elaboration of subjects' responses. A representative sample of pupils was interviewed in each unit. The sampling was based on teachers' perceptions of differences among pupils. The purpose of the observational element in the design was: (a) to familiarise the subjects and researcher with one another, (b) to provide a common source of reference for subsequent interviews, and (c) to offer verification of events described by interviewees.

The Nature and Importance of Commonality

The question of commonality between teacher and pupil perceptions of significant teaching and learning events was a major concern at the outset of this project. We use the term 'commonality' to refer first to similarities in teachers' and pupils' selection of classroom events, and second, to similarities in the ways in which teachers and pupils talk about the same teaching and learning related activities in the lessons we observed.

Our initial worry was that, in response to our non-directive interviewing style, pupils would reveal perceptions that were completely unconnected with those of their teachers, and vice versa. Whilst such a finding would have been of interest in itself, it would still have left important questions unanswered. A complete lack of commonality in perceptions would have told us about differences in the most prominent concerns of teachers and pupils, but would have left us to speculate about commonalities which might be present but less prominent in their perceptions. In order to cater for this eventuality a directive element was added into the interview procedure. Towards the end of interviews which lacked evidence of commonality, examples of events and situations described by teachers as significant were introduced; the same procedure was applied in teacher interviews, using pupils' perceptions.

The second level of commonality refers to teachers' and pupils' ways of talking about teaching and learning. This involves pupils and teachers' talking about their perceptions of the significance of particular events, and the ways in which these relate to successful learning. A key principle here is that of authenticity of subject response. Measures were taken, therefore, to avoid 'leakage' between teacher and pupils responses via the researcher. It is the extent and nature of the similarities and differences between teachers' and pupils' ways of thinking about such events that forms the main focus of the present chapter.

Evidence of Commonality

In the event, the degree of spontaneous commonality between teacher and pupil perceptions was much greater than we expected. This often made it unnecessary to introduce the directive element into the interviews. Where the directive element was employed this often simply added to commonalities that arose spontaneously.

Lesson activities

Commonality of teacher and pupil perceptions is strongest at the descriptive level. Teachers and pupils are in close agreement about the activities engaged in lessons, in general. Where there are *disagreements* here it is usually the result of error, where, for example, the subject is recalling a different lesson. There are, however, interesting differences in the completeness of recall. Teachers tend to recall the events of the lesson sequentially, or in relation to the outcomes they were seeking, whilst pupils sometimes fail to recall events that the teacher has cited. For example, in a history lesson in the 'Medieval Realms' unit, the teacher, Ms Wills, described five different major activities that were carried out in the lesson in the following sequence:

(1) She read to pupils a text on the subject of the conflict between the church and state at the time of Becket.
(2) She instructed the pupils to make a written summary of the text.
(3) She read to the pupils an account of the murder of Becket.
(4) She conducted a question and answer session on the subject of bias in the text.
(5) She told the story of the history of the conflict between Becket and the King.

The pupils who were interviewed after this lesson all gave responses that focused on the account of Becket's murder. Even when prompted they tended to display difficulty in recalling any of the other events of the lesson. Reasons given by pupils for the prominence of this item all focus on the gruesome and lurid nature of the story:

> All the blood and guts — that's really awful: I just remember it by that. [Ken]

> His [Becket's] brains were splattered all over the floor, and that sort of thing, [...] [I remember it] because it was gory. [Frank]

> Today was quite interesting: how he got killed and that. [...] It was interesting how many times he got stabbed and he didn't die. And it was only the fifth time that he died. [...] I'm not into that sort of [gory] thing. It's just the way it's sort of amazing. [Gordon]

There is a response pattern here which repeats itself in all of the classes studied and across the subject boundaries. The classroom events that pupils appear to recall most readily are those which they associate with a state of contemporaneous high arousal. The actual events which are recalled in this way are of a wide variety, including story writing, blackboard work, role play exercises, class discussions and so on. The most commonly recalled events, however, are those which involve the pupils in interactive ways, such as role plays and groupwork, and those which provide cognitive stimulation, such as well read and effective stories, and highly evocative visual stimuli. Often, once such events have been recalled, they appear to act as a cue for the recall of other less arousing events. In extreme cases, such as the Becket lesson, however, the associated state of arousal is so heightened that it appears to interfere with the recall of other less arousing events.

Classroom outcomes

Commonality in relation to classroom outcomes varies in a number of ways. It is possible to classify the types of outcomes talked about by teachers and pupils into two broad categories. The first category is 'Learning outcomes' and the second category is a general category covering social and personal outcomes, and includes perceived states of affairs that teachers and pupils consider to have important consequences for learning.

Learning Outcomes

When speaking about learning outcomes teachers often talk in terms of skills and understanding exhibited by pupils:

Technically em, I think they'd established different ways of drafting: making notes, writing from best, and they began to understand what drafting is. [Ms Jack, English]

I've been pleased with the way the kids have presented their work, looked at their stories, done the things I've asked them to and, in many cases, done more than I've asked them to, and changed their mind and so on, and come up with some — as I see it — hell of an improvement. [Ms Scott, English]

Ms Wills (history) describes with satisfaction the ways in which pupils apply skills they first practised a term earlier, in their study of the Roman Empire, in the Becket lesson:

I was quite pleased with that, they did pick out some quite good things from that [...] we talked about if they were describing Caesar's death would they make it gory or not, depending on which side they were on; I thought they picked on that.

A second history teacher, Ms Bell, describes a similar observation of pupil use of skills:

We talked about reliability of evidence [...]; some of them are getting on quite well with that idea; they are understanding those concepts quite well already.

When pupils talk about learning outcomes they too sometimes talk about skills and understanding:

Mary: I didn't know before this lesson that] when you make a theory, you have to have supporting evidence for it.

Jane: Yes, I didn't know about that before.

I didn't really know about how they [historians] worked [in] history, and how we find out about history. [...] [I now understand that] somebody tells somebody; [...] somebody tells somebody else what happened. The story's going to change. But they go back and find evidence if it's happened like the police do. [James]

In this example the use of the key term 'evidence' reveals a link between the teacher's and pupils' accounts of the outcomes of the lesson:

That [...] kind of questioning approach is just something that I'd certainly like them, as historians, to develop, and to be always thinking about evidence and reliability. [Mr Home]

Other key words that are recurrent in both teacher and pupil accounts include: 'theory', 'story', and 'eliminate'. This indicates that there are important links between teacher input and learning outcomes. This phenomenon recurs throughout the interview transcripts, and can be related to teachers' often deliberate highlighting and reinforcement of specific items of vocabulary, both in English and history.

In another example we see how teacher and pupil perceptions of learning outcomes differ subtly. In this lesson the teacher has given the pupils the task of summarising the causes of Julius Caesar's assassination, as they are represented in a text book, and then ordering them in order of importance. The teacher describes the outcome of the lesson in terms of pupil performance and infers learning outcomes from this:

> I was quite pleased with the way they thought about it, because looking around at the way they'd rearranged the list on their tables, [...] most of them had actually put what I would consider to be the more important ones at the top [...]; they seemed to sort that out in quite a good way. [...] I mean that's just starting them off on the idea that there are lots of reasons for something happening, and that some reasons are more important than others. [Ms Bell]

When Alice [a pupil] was interviewed about this lesson she claimed to have learned:

> Different ways how he was murdered.

She also goes on to describe how certain skills she has developed in the course of this lesson may be of more general benefit in her future historical studies, such as the study of World War II:

> We know how Hitler was killed, but if we didn't, we could do the same thing that we did with Julius Caesar, if he had been murdered. [...] [There are] probably lots of reasons [why Hitler killed himself]. [...] There might just have been one reason. We don't know.

We find Alice's account of outcomes somewhat inconclusive as a means of assessing the extent to which she has achieved the outcomes described by her teacher. On the one hand, her focus is on the literal content of the lesson: she has absorbed knowledge about the causes of Caesar's death. This, however, is an outcome that the teacher does not mention. On the other hand, Alice shares with her teacher a perception of the transferability of the skills she has practised in this lesson. But the 'basic idea', cited by the teacher, that 'there are lots of reasons for something happening' is not as firmly held by Alice as Ms Bell would appear to expect. Alice does not generalise from her study of Caesar's death that there are many reasons for events, rather she believes she has learned a technique for ordering multiple causes in order of importance; it is only 'probable' that other historical events will have multiple causes.

The subtle disparity between Alice's and Ms Bell's accounts of learning outcomes is frequently reflected in other cases. Like Alice, pupils most often talk about their learning in terms of the acquisition of factual information, or in terms of their mastery of instrumental skills. Thus in an English lesson where pupils were instructed to produce their own 'passports' as part of an autobiography, the teacher describes the learning outcomes in terms of pupils' mastery of the drafting process:

> I don't think I've ever been quite as successful. [...] looking at that redraft [produced by pupils], I felt the message had got through. Because what they submitted to me was, for marking, was far superior to what I had got [...] initially from them. [...] So even if it was just on a presentation point of view, or the use of full stops, they had tried very hard to in some way alter their first draft, and produced [...] what [...] was, as I'd asked, 'the best piece of writing you've ever, ever done'. So [...] the idea of drafting, I feel, has been successful.

This is reflected well in pupil accounts. For example, this pupil describes the procedures she has learned about in the lesson:

> You write it in first draft as a list, and then you put it in an order. And then [...], like in rough, you do what you think you should put; so working out what you could write. And then you do the rest. [...] It helps, cos if you write one thing then, and also you think of something else. [...] and if you've got a list, [...] a list of what kind of thing [you might want to write], you just put them, in any order that you think them up, and then you can sort them out into the order you want. [Joan]

Earlier in the same interview, however, a second pupil [Philip] describes the major learning experience of the lesson in terms of learning how to fill in a passport application form 'when we get older [...] [and] we get our own passport'. He too refers later to having employed the drafting process, though as an incidental, instrumental process.

The commonality in teachers' and pupils' ways of speaking about their learning experiences indicates a covergence in their thinking about subjects which is often attributed by pupils to teacher input in lessons, either direct input, through oral and/or visual presentation, or indirect input, through pupil use of resources that the teacher has directed pupils to. The evidence of divergent perceptions of learning outcomes, however, points to the presence of a more active approach to learning among pupils, who, on these occasions, would appear to be engaging in their own sense making activities, independent, to a large extent, of teacher action and direction.

Other Classroom Outcomes

The second category of outcomes relates in particular to classroom states and events which are perceived by teachers and pupils to be productive, in relation to learning or other outcomes. Whilst such events and states might be seen by an observer as 'processes' rather than 'outcomes', they are seen by teachers and pupils as outcomes, that is, as desirable or undesirable end-states. Under this heading are a range of behaviours which are judged by teachers and pupils to relate to learning, pupils' social behaviour, the quality of social interaction and the general social climate in the classroom. Other outcomes relate to pupils' affective states, both inferred from pupil behaviour and as experienced by pupils, and the products of classroom processes, such as pupils' verbal performance and other 'work' products. Teachers, in particular, also employ a concept of 'progress', in relation to the quality of work and the rate at which it is done in the classroom.

An important criterion applied by teachers and pupils when talking about the success of a particular lesson is the notion of 'working well'. Whether or not pupils are 'working well' is often determined on the basis of observed or self-reported behaviour. 'Working well' involves engaging in on-task behaviour in an appropriate way. Ms Wills (history) provides us with an example of how such on-task behaviour is sometimes associated with pupil learning and understanding. She is describing the pupils' performance in the question and answer session she conducted after her reading of the story of Becket's murder:

> I was quite pleased with that; they did pick out some quite good things from that. [...] when we did those newspapers for English, we talked about the language bias and the word 'murder' had come out before as a very loaded word. So [in the lesson on Becket] they'd remembered that, which was good.

Sometimes, however, 'working well' can be quite independent of desired learning outcomes, as Ms Bell (history) shows:

> The story of Romulus and Remus — I want to do it how I did it before, which was to divide the class up into groups of four, [...] and then in their groups they carve up the story into sections. And what we ended up with was a piece of sugar paper with four A4 sheets on, with a picture and caption underneath in the right order, and told the story of Romulus and Remus. And that worked very well. I was very pleased with how they did that last year, and so I'm going to try that again with some sort of extra explanation about paying attention to the story, because there were some rather strange pictures that came out of it where they obviously hadn't listened very well.

Here, although what we might term the cognitive outcomes of the task are somewhat unsatisfactory, the task is still considered by the teacher to have 'worked very well', so much so that she intends to repeat the task with her current Year 7 class. In this case it is the teacher's belief that the pupils are engaging with the task in an appropriate way, and are enjoying the work, that are the main sources of satisfaction. When she comes to repeat the lesson with her current Year 7 groups she takes measures to improve her telling of the story and so enhance the learning outcomes to be gained from the lesson.

Discussion, group and pair work sessions are often judged in similar ways by teachers of both subjects, with criteria such as pupil 'liveliness', willingness to participate, and responsiveness being employed by teachers. Pupils and teachers share a concern for the importance of discipline and listening skills in group discussion, as well as a recognition of the need for a balance between the distribution of time between teacher and pupil talk. Pupils complain when teachers 'go on for too long', whilst teachers often claim to deliberately ration their talking time:

> I actually do try not to lecture children too much, because once I start, that's me — I can go on forever. So it's something I try not to do much. [...] they all switch off. [Ms Bell]

Some teachers place enormous stress on the process of teaching, and the way in which this contributes to the social climate of the classroom, as well as their pupils' perceptions of the subject being taught. The issue of teacher talk is seen as central to this, and can even be seen to influence the lesson content that the teacher selects. Ms Bell illustrates this point, when she talks about what she experiences as a tension between the emphasis placed by National Curriculum history on historical skills as opposed to content. Whilst she recognises the need to make pupils aware of the skills they are using, she is concerned that pupils' enthusiasm for the subject might be undermined by an over emphasis on what she sees as the dry and over abstract nature of skill analysis:

> If I start going on [to pupils] about, 'well, of course, you realise what we've been doing is a historical skill'. And then launch into this long [lecture], they all switch off. I don't want them to do that, because I don't want them to think that history's got to be laboured.

As a consequence of this way of thinking, Ms Bell decides to leave dormant the issue of which skills pupils have been practising in the work on the death of Caesar:

> I think that even if I'm not quite happy [that] I've said enough about it [the skills practised], I don't think I'm going to go on about it anymore, because I think it's time for them to move on to the next bit of work.

Ms Bell is content to leave this issue until they revisit it at a later date:

> They're going to be doing this in Year 8 and 9, and gradually they understand. I can say to the Year 9s now, 'look, we've been doing this since first year. What skill are we doing?'

Pupils often share with teachers a common view of what it means to 'work well', citing the ways in which pupils 'get on with one another' in groups, and the extent to which group and pair discussions focus on the set task. Pupils often describe criteria for the quality of group experience: good groups being ones where pupils cooperate with one another, listen to one another, maintain a focus on the task and divide responsibilities fairly. An important quality sought in fellow group members and claimed by many interviewees for themselves is the willingness to accept unattractive roles and responsibilities, in order to promote group progress. Teachers do not tend to talk about group membership qualities in such detail, tending to employ more global perspectives, and focusing on the outward indications of pupil cooperation and involvement.

Sometimes the appropriate functioning of group processes is seen as an end in itself, by both teachers and pupils, as is demonstrated by Ms Pitt (English) and one of her pupils, in their descriptions of key aspects of one of their lessons:

Some of them [the pupils] have no opinions and would give in very easily [during negotiations with fellow group members]. But I noticed that they were refusing to do so. And I think that is quite a positive thing. But then also, some of them — like Marjory for instance was willing to compromise, which I've never seen her do before. In the last project she wanted to run it her way. [Ms Pitt]

Well, in English today, …last week in our reports we all wrote what we really felt. And some of us had a bit of trouble working in groups and cooperating. And the idea of today's lesson was to help you overcome those and cooperate with everybody else. […] [The lesson] helped me cooperate a bit more in mixed sexes, cos I don't normally go with girls; I normally stick with boys. [Charles]

Here the commonality of perception of the central focus of the lesson would seem to have a strong relationship to the fact that Charles is able to place the lesson in sequence with an earlier lesson.

Both pupils and teachers stress the importance of pupils' affective states, as they are observed and experienced in lessons. Both teachers and pupils will often refer to pupil enjoyment, or the experience of 'fun' as important outcomes which can lead to effective learning. Ms Bell gives an example of this when she describes the way she has used an extract from the script of 'Monty Python's Life of Brian' to introduce the study of the Roman Empire:

I do try quite hard to get them to enjoy their work, and I think sometimes if they have a bit of fun along the way, then they enjoy it and hopefully it sticks a bit more, […] hopefully they'll also realise that there is something serious about it as well.

It is interesting to note the relative weighting here between the teacher's recognition of the 'fun' aspect of the chosen resource material and her tentativeness with regard to its efficacy as a learning aid. An English teacher, Ms Brown, declares the importance of pupil 'enjoyment' to be such that she ranks it among her major teaching objectives:

> I want to teach them that English is interesting and dynamic […]. I am also trying to teach them to do research. […] I am not sorry, and also just to enjoy it!

All of the teachers in the study express similar sentiments at different times, and suggest that they see part of their role as being an ambassador for their subjects, with a responsibility to present it in a positive and attractive light to their pupils. The pupils also share a concern with the 'fun' aspects of their learning experience. This will be dealt with in greater detail in a later section.

Teaching methods and strategies

Both teachers and pupils are deeply concerned with the means by which learning is facilitated in the classroom. There is strong agreement between teachers and pupils about the range of most effective teacher strategies and techniques. However, there are also important variations in the detailed perceptions of teachers and pupils which are likely to have consequences for teacher effectiveness.

Pupils and teachers both describe situations in which the following methods are valuable as aids to learning and understanding:

- Teacher making explicit the agenda for the lesson.
- Teacher recapping on previous lesson; highlighting continuity between lessons.
- Story telling (by teacher).*
- Reading aloud (by teacher/by pupils).
- Teacher mediation and modification of pupil verbal input to class discussion/board work.
- Oral explanation by teacher, often combined with (a) discussion/question answer sessions; (b) use of blackboard.*
- Blackboard notes and diagrams as aide memoire.
- Use of pictures and other visual stimuli (for exploration/information).*
- use of 'models' based on pupil work or generated by teacher.
- Structure for written work generated and presented by teacher.
- Group/pair work (for oral and practical purposes).*
- Drama/role play.*
- Printed text/worksheets.

- Use of stimuli which relates to pupil pop-culture.*
- Pupil drawing (mentioned by pupils only).

However, whilst many pupils favour certain of these methods (the items followed by an asterisk) as particularly *powerful* learning aids, the teachers tend not to see these as distinctive. Rather, the teachers tend to take a more contextualised view, seeing different methods as being appropriate for different learning tasks, and being appropriate for reasons relating to prevailing conditions (such as: time, nature and availability of resources, perceptions of the class, classroom management considerations, their view of the nature of their subject).

The difference between teachers' and pupils' ways of looking at the issue of teaching methods can be summarised in the following terms: pupils have preferred ways of engaging with and acquiring new knowledge and understanding, and these preferences are perceived by them to relate to the success of the learning experience; for teachers, on the other hand, the choice of teaching method is governed by a range of sometimes conflicting considerations, which may or may not relate to pupils' preferred approaches to learning. This means that teachers are sometimes employing methods which are not, in their view, most appropriate to the material. Ms Wills illustrates this point:

> I can't afford to give more than this week to Thomas Becket. And anyway that's too much, because we've only got two weeks [until the end of term]. I'm going to have to devise ways of dealing with Magna Carta and the Peasants' Revolt fairly speedily. [...] we're supposed to be doing the origins of parliament and the legacy of the Middle Ages. [...] how do I get all that done in such a small space of time? [...] Oh, I shan't do it [all]. I'll probably show them a video of the Peasants' Revolt, or something. [I have to] make a decision about that. But it is a lot of pressure really.

The more immediate classroom context is also a powerful influence on teachers' choice of approach. This is illustrated by Ms Hall (English), who describes her reasons for shifting from a task combining reading and a whole class discussion to written work on the same subject (a narrative version of *The Tempest*):

> I think it's fascinating [...] their response when I said, 'right, [...] we'll leave it there and do some writing'. 'Oooh!' [imitation of pupils' groans] As if you'd asked them to do the worst thing in the world. [...] But I'm aware — I suppose it's classroom management — [...] You become aware that some children have gone past the stage of wanting to hear what other people's ideas are. [...] Just a few who were — people like Jimmy, who were obviously restless from the word go [...] and the

odd other few, who were getting a bit fidgety. I felt it was time to actually get them to focus on writing something down.

In this example, Ms Hall's reasons for changing the task are not entirely related to the pupils' waning interest, but also to other pupils' apparent over enthusiasm for the topic:

> Quite a few of them were getting restless because they were excited about what they were doing [...] and were obviously enjoying it. They were just going to get more and more high. And it would be hard to pull them back down to write down their homework, let alone write anything else down.

Another important consideration is the teacher's perceptions of the nature of the lesson content, as Ms Wills again illustrates:

> I think any topic that involves issues, I would try to teach in a way that they were actually thinking for themselves, and making decisions about what they thought about it. I mean, you can't really do that sort of thing with medieval farming, can you!

Similarly, Ms Hall accounts for her increased use of group work and greater exercise of pupil autonomy in terms of the topic of study

> It's because of the nature of what they're doing. [...] that's the easiest way to do it. I mean the soap opera work was [...] at the start [...] didactic in terms of, 'OK, [...] what's a soap opera? What do you know about soap operas?' And it was only during that soap opera work that the tables changed [i.e. the arrangement of desks in the classrooms was changed to facilitate greater pupil interaction than was permitted under the previous arrangement].

Thus we find that teachers employ each of the methods listed above at different times in accordance with their perceptions of appropriateness in relation to the prevailing conditions. It should be stressed that some teachers include in these conditions assumptions about pupils' learning processes, as Ms Jack (English) shows, when she talks about the use of classroom talk with her Year 7 group:

> Through talk, you make more specific in your own mind, so you clarify in your own mind what it is you wish to say [...]. And I think that's happened with the children.

Another English teacher, Mr Fox, describes the way in which he seeks to provide learning experiences which cater for a wide range of pupil aptitudes:

> I always like to address the three profile components through every unit of work I do. There's got to be an element of reading, there's got to be an element of speaking and listening, there's got to be an element

of writing [...]. If we're defining mixed ability in terms of those who find writing difficult, then on the other hand, those who are competent oral communicators, then there'll be something in every new approach for every different member of the group. So for example they won't be saddled with the restrictions that writing imposes [...] Sometimes they'll be freed from that and they'll be in small groups talking or improvisation sessions, [or in groups] where some of them will be text bound, so they'll be reading. So it might allow the strong readers to extend themselves, and sometimes they won't be bound by texts, so it'll allow those children who find reading very difficult to be liberated from that and to just improvise. So I hope that [...] a variety of approach is [...] going to allow every member of the class to be involved with it in some way.

Mr Fox's pragmatic solution acknowledges the variety that is likely to exist in pupils' preferred approaches to learning, whilst taking as its starting point the contextual matter of the linguistic skills that are prescribed by the National Curriculum.

Pupils' judgements of the effectiveness of teaching methods relate almost exclusively to their personal experiences of learning. There are strong themes running through these pupil accounts which indicate that pupils have good reasons for favouring certain teaching methods over others. It has already been noted (see section on lesson activities) that pupils recall more readily lesson activities that they associate with a relatively high level of arousal. Pupils' accounts of their own most effective learning are associated with these same events. Invariably pupils describe a high degree of constructive participation in the events recalled. Accounts of such participation often reveal important links between the activities engaged in and pupils' knowledge and understanding of lesson content. In these circumstances, therefore, the learning that has taken place is linked to events in which the pupils have participated in some way, such as in a physical or imaginative sense. This is demonstrated vividly in the often cited dramatic reconstruction of the assassination of Julius Caesar, staged by Ms Bell's class. Here we see how a pupil's (Grant) knowledge and understanding of this subject is linked to his recall of classroom events in which he has participated:

We done about the killing of Julius Caesar, the assassination of Julius Caesar, and we done it in a sort of like play [...] in the classroom. We put all the tables back and we done all the speaking and that. Yeah, and I was one of the crowd. [...] it was good, because everyone had brought sheets in and dressed up as Romans. [...] I knew [ie. learned] from that that they didn't want a king, because [they wanted] to stop Rome from going under again. [...] Before they'd had a king and queen, [and] they got a bit big for their boots, and they killed them, or something, and I didn't know that. And I knew that he [Caesar] was really brutally killed, because all the senate gathered round him and they each drew their daggers and stabbed him, and it said on something that he was stabbed twenty eight times.

The close association between the new knowledge and the setting and people with whom Grant is personally involved is clearly demonstrated:

There was Terry, I think was Brutus, and he done a defence, why he killed Julius Caesar. And everybody liked him. And then John Anthony [sic] I think it was, came on and he sort of like slowly went against Brutus [...]. and all the crowd ended up against him. And they went off saying that they'd burn his house and that. It was good! [...] I [am] sort of like remembering Simon standing up on the chair, speaking out, and I remember two people dragging on Julius Caesar, and I can remember Tracy, that was John [sic] Anthony — I can remember her showing the dagger wounds, because we had this special sheet that has dagger wounds in it. And another thing I learned from it was Julius Caesar's final words: 'Et tu Brute'. Which means, 'and you Brutus', [...] because he thought Brutus was his best friend. And Brutus ended up killing him; so he didn't like that very much!

Grant firmly believes that although some of his knowledge of this topic has been gathered from reading, that reading alone would have been ineffective. It is the drama which is the focal point of his appreciation of this topic; the reading is only valuable in a supplementary sense:

Well, you take more notice when you [are] doing it in a play, than you do when you're sat there reading it. So you really listen hard, and it helps a lot.

An important feature of this account is the way in which Grant's description of apparently irrelevant incidental details forms part of his recall. It is suggested that such incidental features provide important cues by which he is able to link the subject knowledge he describes to his personal experience of taking part in a real event.

Grant's account of the role play of the death of Caesar is typical of pupil responses to this lesson, which is repeatedly referred to by many pupils long after it has taken place. In fact there had been a ten week gap between the lesson and Grant's account of it reported here. Clearly, the sheer extreme nature of the events portrayed in this example might be assumed to be an important cause here. However, we find similar effects with dramatisations of less sensational material, such as a role play in which the division of Roman society into Plebeians and Patricians was enacted; the use of role play by an English teacher to demonstrate the appropriateness of register in face to face communication; the use of role play by another English teacher to portray the story lines of a series of narrative poems, and a role play in which pupils were required to discuss the pros and cons of taking part in the Peasants' Revolt. This would indicate that it is the method rather than the content that is the critical factor.

Another highly inventive use of role play was by Mr Fox, an English teacher. Unknown to the rest of the class, he instructed two pupils to role play an argument and fight at the beginning of the lesson. The role play ended with one of the pupils defying Mr Fox and leaving the room. Mr Fox describes the purpose of the role play as a stimulus for pupil talk about a real event, in order to address the concept of 'register' in language. Felicity and Barbara describe their experience and learning in lesson in the following terms:

> **Felicity:** They did this sort of play thing […]. Two boys came rushing in and bashed into the tables and were fighting. And Albert said, 'shut up!' to Mr Fox. And we had to witness what they said […]. Out of the classroom we had to witness what they said and everything. And he [Mr Fox] wrote them down on the board. And [we had to] interview each other. […] And we found out that in the playground, you'd be talking slang, but if the headmaster was talking [i.e. 'if we were talking to the headmaster'], it would be more standard English. […]
>
> **Barbara:** I thought it [the 'fight'] was serious, and that it was the real thing [at first] […]
>
> **Felicity:** If we thought it was a set up, we wouldn't have…
>
> **Barbara:** Put much interest into it.
>
> **Felicity:** Yeah.
>
> **Barbara:** Because we thought it was real, we sort of paid interest, and wanted to talk about it and everything.

Clearly Mr Fox's aim has been achieved with these two girls, whose understandings of the content of the lesson are clearly dependent on their direct experience of the events around which it was based.

These girls' views of the power of role play in the classroom and Grant's enthusiasm and evident absorption in the Julius Caesar lesson, are echoed in relation to other teaching methods and classroom experiences described by pupils as being successful. This is particularly true of their descriptions of the use of storytelling and visual stimuli as teaching aids. In both cases these are seen to have a powerful effect on pupils' learning and understanding.

There are two major categories of stories told by teachers which pupils find effective: stories which are intrinsically interesting by virtue of their content, and stories which appear to reveal something of the personal lives of their teachers. In both cases pupils are motivated to pay close attention by their desire for more information and the entertainment value of the experience. With regard to teachers' personal stories, this applies equally well to teachers' brief personal anecdotes which are often used to illustrate a point. When recalling information pupils often do so most effectively when they follow the narrative patterns of the story as presented by the teacher. It would seem that the sequencing and other structural features of stories provide important cues for recall. Once again, this can be illustrated through the use of highly evocative material, such as the story of the murder of Becket, and by less dramatic means, for example, a personal story told by Ms Wills to illustrate the concepts of short term and long term consequences. This latter story is recalled by several pupils who when defining the nature of short and long term consequences do so by reconstructing events in the teacher's story.

The use of visual stimuli works in a similar way to that of story and drama in that it often seems to provide pupils with a framework by which they are able to recall information. The framework is retained because it links in some way with pupils' existing experience, knowledge, understandings or interests. The unit on the Black Death provides an interesting illustration of this point, showing how a pupil's close examination of a pictorial source stimulates his thinking about the subject, and how the combination of text and picture helps him to extend his knowledge (the picture is from a contemporaneous source and depicts Death as a skeleton riding a horse):

> Well, the first thing I looked at was the skeleton, and I thought, 'ugh! he doesn't look very nice'. [...] Then I looked all around the edges, and there was some rich people dying, and there was some holy people dying, reverends and stuff. And then on the other side, there was sort of like dark, in a dark colour; there was poor people dying. And he was riding on a horse, and the horse was trying to trample on the people as well, because the horse was jumping about all over. I noticed that all the streets were dirty, and some people, I think it was the Germans, thought it was a message from God, saying they hadn't behaved themselves properly. [...] After people had read their sources [ie. pupils read sections of the textbook aloud to the class] I started to look more closely [at the picture, for] fountains with dirty water and that. [Ken]

Visual representation is not simply important in relation to the nature of stimuli material, it is itself a major element in the cognitive processes which some pupils report employing during learning. Frank provides a vivid example of this, when he describes the way in which he responded to the teacher's reading of the story of Becket's murder:

> [while Ms Wills was reading the story I was] just like making pictures in my head of it, of what was happening. I was sort of thinking about Feddlestone [local village] church. I don't know why! [...] Picturing the church helps me know the scene and what's happening better. [...] I remember four knights meeting and a man, he was a man and not a knight, [...] he come down from some stairs, or come from a door, stood by a post. And they tried to drag him away, but they couldn't get him away from the post.

Ken describes a similar technique:

> Well, [when] she's reading it out I was thinking about what it would have been like, and [...] when something interesting comes up I put that in my kind of play [...], [When the teacher told a story about a car crash] I did the same again, put myself in a car crash, went to court. And then we did it again with the Black Death, I did the same.

Both of these pupils are describing their own ways of making sense of learning material. In both cases they transform the teacher's input into their own terms of reference. In the first case the pupil consciously draws on his own experience to create a setting for the story of Becket's murder. In the second example the pupil enters into the story imaginatively.

The theme of transformation is powerful in pupil accounts. When it occurs it usually involves pupils forging connections between their past or present experience and teacher input. In the accounts of drama/role play activities, pictorial representation and story telling we find pupils engaging in what might be termed a process of *concretisation*, whereby ideas which teachers present are made distinct and given a meaning which is dependent on the context of their delivery; sometimes this context is chiefly provided by the teacher, other times by the pupils. In either case, however, the pupils engage *actively* in the process, by constructing the context (as with visualisation techniques), or by bringing their experience and interest into focus (as in story telling, the use of visual aids and role play). The chief activity that pupils seem to be engaging in is perhaps best termed one of *appropriation*. The activity of appropriation will now be further exemplified in relation to the remaining teaching methods that pupils identify as being distinctive in their effectiveness.

Whilst drama/role play, story telling and visual stimuli, are considered by pupils to be important for their imaginative, visual and activity content, class discussion, teacher-led question and answer situations, and group/pairwork are taken together because of the importance that pupils place on their own verbal participation in these classroom practices. Once again, however, the accent is on the ways in which these contribute to pupil appropriation and construction of knowledge. From the pupil standpoint, the most valuable shared aspects of these approaches are the opportunities they create for pupils to generate and be exposed to new representations of knowledge and ideas, as well as providing possible confirmation or denial of their own ideas.

According to pupils, the most successful class discussions are often those which provide opportunities for autonomous thought and personal expression whilst being carefully directed by the teacher. The most striking examples of discussion were cited by pupils from English lessons. Emily and Sean talk with great enthusiasm, at great length and in considerable detail about one of Ms Hall's lessons. The lesson was based around a prose version of *The Tempest* (by Ian Serrallier). Ms Hall justified her selection of the topic on the basis of the National Curriculum's demand for pupils to study pre-twentieth century literature. Her strategy is to concentrate on the plot of the play and to introduce extracts from the original Shakespeare text at certain points throughout the unit. She has been guided in her choice of strategy by a concern that pupils might find reading the play in its original form a too difficult and unstimulating task. In this and the previous lesson the whole class has followed the prose version whilst the teacher reads it aloud. At certain points the teacher stops reading and asks the pupils questions about the plot. On several occasions the teacher uses these breaks in the reading to encourage pupils to a share speculations as to how the plot will develop:

> I like it how we're reading it, step by step, rather than just reading it all. [...] So you can, like, really get into the story and guess what could happen next. It's more fun, rather than just reading page by page. There's more adventure in it, like the books we were reading in the library. [Emily]

Emily is referring here to a series of books in which the reader is required to make choices which determine the particular way in which the narrative develops. She finds a sense of 'adventure' in this approach to the story. The 'adventure' lies in the mental challenge of unravelling the mystery of the story and in the possibility of confirmation or denial of their hypotheses as the story unfolds. The theme of pupil involvement is strong here. The fact that pupils are required to articulate their ideas in the discussion phase, also acts as a stimulus for developing and fixing their ideas:

> Well, when she was reading, I thought of an idea, and then, when we were asked to do it [i.e. to give their ideas], it sort of really pinged up!

The most important aspect of this situation, however, is the discussion itself which acts as a stimulus to pupil thinking:

> [whenever we stopped reading] I was thinking, like what was going to happen next. Because we started, like, where say something strange happened, and new people came into the story, and discussed what they'd be. And people [other pupils, came] with ideas of what's going to happen next. [...] [Other pupils] were asking questions. Like they'll remind us about something that happened at the beginning [of the story], and they'll go, 'oh yeah, that happened'. And when they gave the ideas it gave you one as well; to help you to what you were thinking. [Sean]

This genuine sharing of ideas helps pupils to deepen their knowledge and understanding of the text, by encouraging them to reflect on and develop their own ideas:

> **Emily:** It's good, I prefer lessons like that instead of just, like, doing work from a book, because I like discussions and things.
>
> **Sean:** Yeah. Because you can see other people's point of view about the story and share your own [view]. [...]
>
> **Emily:** [I enjoyed having] other people agree with you, and [when] they thought it was a good idea [...] [if they didn't agree with you] they would explain why they didn't think it was a good idea, and all that, and I wouldn't have thought of that, so I would agree with them.

Group consensus is also seen as a way of eliminating some ideas:

> If someone says something and the rest of the class doesn't agree [...] it puts some ideas out of the way, and then you'll be left with a few; so you might come up with an idea.

Emily and Sean exemplify the way in which their own thinking is developed through discussion, both with reference to the lesson, and through a demonstration in the course of the interview. They are referring to a section of the lesson in which they were discussing why Prospero should want to send Ariel to bring Ferdinand to him:

> **Emily:** One [pupil] was saying, [...] 'so that they could like kidnap him'. [...] Somebody else had an idea, like he [Ferdinand] could marry my [Prospero's daughter] if you [Ferdinand] tell me about your dad: where he is and everything. So he could find out and then he could go and get her. So I've got your son trapped, so let me have my throne back...
>
> **Sean:** Yeah, but he [Ferdinand] didn't know that Prospero was there. He thought that Prospero was dead, ages ago. Because it said like [in the text], twelve years later, when Caliban — six years later — so it was

a long time after. He'd forgotten about his brother, and didn't know what he looked like so...

Emily: And Prospero loved his daughter, so I don't think he would have done that to her: like, make her fall in love with Ferdinand.

Emily's starting point in this extract is her recollection of a contribution made to the lesson by an unnamed pupil. This stimulates Sean to cite textual detail which might support the hypothesis. Emily, however, responds to Sean by presenting an opposing view based on her recall of the text. This extract strongly supports the claim of the effectiveness of discussion as a means of encouraging pupils to formulate and articulate ideas on the basis of a close reading of text. The pupils' automatic slipping into discussion mode during the interview indicates the power of this technique: these pupils are clearly highly stimulated by the activity and show an exuberance in their performance of this skill.

Another interesting feature of this extract is the way in which Emily, in the opening lines, quickly switches from the use of the third person to the first person when describing Prospero's possible motives, indicating the extent of her imaginative involvement with the text, and hinting at the type of cognitive process that she may employ in approaching these questions. This offers support to assertions that have already been made about the way in which some pupils appear to 'concretise' ideas. The elements of fun and active engagement, that these pupils reveal, are not to be under-estimated as factors contributing to the success of this strategy.

Group work and pair work operate in very similar ways to discussion, though there are important distinctions to be made. Whilst the patterns of interaction and the progress of work are structured by the teacher in whole class discussions, in groupwork pupils take responsibility for these areas, and the extent to which pupils are successful in dealing with these forms an important part of both teachers' and pupils' perceptions of the success of group work. As Clive suggests in his description of an English lesson in which his group is required to devise and write a play script:

[Our group worked] quite well, actually. Because we got a lot done, and we figured what we were doing in the story straight away. There was no arguing about the title.

Pupils are virtually unanimous in describing the major value of group work as being, like class discussion, that it widens the pool of available ideas, and through this, enables pupils to advance their thinking in ways which they could not achieve alone. As Clive again puts it:

It's not as boring as working on your own [...] when you're in groups [...] you get different ideas, whereas if you're on your own, you've just got one idea, and the first idea you get you just put down really.

Clive demonstrates this when he describes the ways in which the group came to devise the eventual title, and how this discussion led to substantive developments in the plot of their play:

Another title, that Brendan said, it was about 'Murder at Crinkley Bottom'. So we got the name of the place, Crinkley Bottom, to put in the story. And then, just as Brendan was writing it, Ian thought about 'Murder that I Wrote'. And then we said, 'Murder We Wrote'. [...] [We] just thought it was a better title to put in it.

This use of the multiple perspectives provided by group members is also manifested in other ways, such as in the mediation of teacher input to group processes. There are several examples provided by pupils, in which different pupils contribute to the group at different times an input based upon instruction given by the teacher earlier in the lesson. In this way the group acts as a kind of super-memory on which the group draws as the need arises, with each pupil being custodian of a slightly different set of recollections of teacher or other input.

Pairwork is experienced as having similar benefits to group work, with the exception that it is more often cited as offering pupils a personal rehearsal function, in that they are often required to use pairwork for purposes of articulating ideas and hypotheses prior to some form of written or oral performance. Both pair work and group work also provide pupils with opportunities for informal peer tutoring, which they find extremely valuable, particularly when they are having difficulties:

The people in the group help me [...] if like I get lost on something they'll help [...]. I was doing something, back in the Romans, and I was going on and I copied the wrong piece of work: got lost in the writing, and that sort of thing, and I said [to other members of the group], 'help put me straight'. [...] they noticed what I was doing wrong.

A powerful feature uniting all of these preferred strategies is the opportunities they all provide for pupils to represent information in ways that they find personally meaningful. This is true of the more personal modes, such as imaginative enactment and visualisation, and of the more social/verbal strategies, such as discussion and groupwork. A commonly repeated claim by pupils, for example, is that where pupils have difficulty understanding points presented by teachers, they often benefit from hearing the same point rephrased by a fellow pupil in terms that are more familiar to them. This also works in the opposite way sometimes, with teachers 'refining' pupils' verbal contributions and making their ideas more accessible to the rest of the group. Similarly, teachers' questions sometimes enable pupils to articulate understandings of which they were not conscious.

The final strategy to be dealt with in this section is that of 'drawing'. This strategy is not generally highly valued by the teachers in this study, but it is considered to be a valuable learning medium by some pupils, particularly in history. There are repeated references to detailed knowledge of various historical situations that pupils attribute to their experience of having drawn them. Examples of this include knowledge about Roman villas, Roman weapons and battle tactics. It is suggested that 'drawing' combines many of the qualities which have been attributed to other favoured strategies, in that it involves the representation of information in the pupil's own (graphic) terms, it involves visual representation, and it requires the active participation of pupils. The importance of this active aspect of pupils' response to learning is underlined by Ken, when he says:

[English and history] they're better than most subjects where you're not doing anything. [They're] like games and design and technology.

This view, however, does not accord with that expressed by the teachers. English and history teachers see themselves as *drawing on* strategies which involve pupils in practical ways when appropriate to the subject matter under consideration. Their subjects are defined by their content, not the method. And as a method, drawing would appear to be one of limited value in the eyes of teachers. We might speculate that this omission has something to do with the non-verbal quality of drawing which distinguishes it from the other agreed strategies.

Learning Problems

It is necessary at this point to make brief reference to some dissenting voices among the pupil group. There is a small subset of pupils who are defined by their teachers as 'high fliers' or 'very able' pupils who report finding some of the strategies discussed above unhelpful and even a hindrance to their learning. For example, there is general agreement between teachers and pupils about the value of teacher reading aloud. Teachers and pupils agree that the teacher's reading often aids pupil comprehension by helping pupils to circumvent possible decoding difficulties, and that their use of expression also helps to elucidate meaning. Many pupils describe the way in which the teacher's reading provides them with a model which enables them to make greater sense of a text when they come to read it themselves. In this situation each subsequent reading adds to the foundation of understanding fostered by the teacher's reading. During the teacher's reading many pupils formulate impressions which are later filled out by their own readings. Some pupils, however, including some of those in the 'more able' set, describe this practice as irritating, and complain that it interferes with their personal interpretations and cognitive representations of a text. Similarly, teachers' use of multiple exemplification, in whatever form, comes in for criticism from these same pupils, who complain at the redundancy of much of it for them.

A second subset of pupils consists of some of those pupils who have learning difficulties in the fields of writing (in particular) and/or reading. Many of these pupils have well developed oral and cognitive skills, but are frustrated by the use of literacy skills as instruments of learning. Consequently, where teachers require pupils to demonstrate understanding or knowledge or cognitive skills through the use of reading or (particularly) writing skills, these pupils are foiled. Whilst their more literate counterparts will often talk about the cognitive aspects of such lessons, with little or no reference to the instrumental use of literacy skills, the pupils with literacy problems focus almost entirely on the technicalities involved. For many of these pupils, every lesson that requires them to write something is to them simply a lesson about writing. This applies not only to those pupils who are officially described as having 'learning difficulties', but relates, in different degrees, to pupils outside this group whose skills are often inadequate to the tasks presented.

It is interesting to note that *all* of the teachers in this study show an awareness of this problem. However, whilst they employ many varied and sophisticated strategies for dealing with reading problems, they show less confidence in their approach to writing problems. Pupils and teachers agree on the efficacy of such teacher strategies as: teacher reading aloud, paired and shared reading, and teacher highlighting of salient parts of texts. There are only isolated examples of pupils claiming to be helped by teachers with their writing. When it occurs this help often takes one of three forms: the teacher rehearses orally the writing that is to be done, the teacher provides a written structure on the blackboard on which pupils model their writing, and the teacher acts as scribe whilst the pupil dictates. Pupil coping strategies include forms of peer tutoring (which sometimes involves straightforward copying or slight modification of a peer's work) and what one pupil [Frank] describes as 'sensing'. When Frank 'senses' that blackboard notes are intended for later transcription, he immediately copies them into his book whilst they are being prepared, so as to avoid the problem of 'falling behind' which results from the confusions he experiences when required to deal with large passages of text.

The issue of the role of literacy skills in learning is an important one, and is a concern shared by teachers as well as pupils. Teachers of both subjects are aware of the difficulties faced by some pupils in terms of literacy. Some of these teachers are also concerned at their own professional socialisation, which has given some of them what they perceive as an over reliance on the use of such skills for instrumental purposes:

> I'm not sure they've understood the issue. [...] And maybe I shouldn't have bothered about any written work at all. I mean, I've got a bit of a hang up over written work. I suppose because I started my teaching career in the days of O level. [...] I find it quite difficult to say, 'hang on a minute, there's no need for them to have a written record of this'. You know, we could have just spent the whole lesson (on reflection now) just doing it through role play, and understanding the issue. [Ms Wills]

Here we have an example of a teacher who reflects that a more effective way of fostering pupil learning would have been to use a strategy which many pupils appear to favour, instead of employing a strategy which has a handicapping effect on some pupils. A further dimension to this problem relates to ways in which teachers of both English and history believe that the National Curriculum through its assessment arrangements and the sheer weight of content in history, is likely to push them further away from teaching approaches which stress pupil activity and involvement, and towards more formal, directive and literacy based approaches to teaching.

Theories of learning

There are three key themes which recur in both teachers' talk about their teaching and pupils' talk about learning. These are:

- the importance of pupil enjoyment and involvement;
- the importance of good social relations between teachers and pupils;
- the importance of pupil autonomy and ownership in learning.

Whilst teachers and pupils are in agreement about the need for these elements to be present, there is a difference in the degree to which pupils and teachers see these as *necessary* conditions for effective learning to take place.

By and large teachers see these factors as contributing to the general social climate of the classroom. The following teacher remarks are typical, showing a concern for pupils' affective states, but only hinting at vague associations between this and pupil learning:

> I think sometimes if they have a bit of fun along the way, then they enjoy it, and hopefully it sticks a bit more. [Ms Bell, history]

> I think you need to have kids on your side and they've got to look forward to what you're going to do. So I think I just try and stress the positive nature of starting a lesson. So it's — on the one hand treading

a fine line between quite a sort of a jolly start and actually geeing up a little bit of excitement, for the kids to say, 'yes, here we go again', you know, 'this is going to be good', and trying to present the task in a fairly positive sort of way. But on the other hand, of course, remembering why we're here. [Mr Fox, English]

Activities which practically involve pupils (such as drama and role play or poster making), and measures which have the effect of heightening pupils' sense of autonomy and ownership of classroom events, are considered desirable because of the positive effect they have on pupil engagement and morale. Similarly, good quality teacher pupil relationships are viewed by teachers as creating a positive tone in the classroom which provides a setting which is conducive to good communication between teacher and pupils.

Pupils, on the other hand, in their detailed descriptions of classroom events suggest that these factors are integral to effective learning. In extreme cases where these features are absent pupils claim to expend minimum attention, if any at all, on the subject matter. The importance of the discrepancy between teacher and pupil perceptions lies in the fact that there are occasions when teachers prefer teaching approaches (such as lecturing) which contravene these principles on the basis of the particular nature of the subject matter to be taught or because of prevailing conditions (e.g. lack of time). There are examples, therefore, of situations in which pupils come out of such lessons with little or no recollection or understanding of what has taken place, and offering merely global accounts such as: 'it was boring; I don't remember much about it'.

On the positive side, we find clear examples of the ways in which the presence of these elements is seen to be a major factor in the learning process. Ken provides an example of this, in his description of his mental activity during the lesson on the murder of Becket. The major stimulus here is the teacher's reading of the story, whilst the pupils have the closed book in front of them. Ken finds the story so 'exciting' that:

I was thinking, 'I've got to read it! I've got to read it! And I've got to see the picture'.

Ken's personal motives are associated with the gruesome quality of the story, and he longs to get the chance to look at the book himself in order to relive this excitement and perhaps obtain further excitement. Ken claims that the story 'really got your mind going'. As a result of this he engages in multiple readings of the text, in an attempt to absorb as much as he can for his own purposes as well as to answer written questions on the topic. His own enthusiasm is clearly instrumental in this process, enabling him, through the use of his imaginative processes, to appropriate and retain knowledge and understanding of the topic:

> I imagined a little bit when Henry II, when he had his fits. [...] If he [Henry II] got his way he'd chop your head off or something.

Similarly, as we have already seen, other activities which pupils see as being 'fun' and allowing their active involvement, such as drama and role play, are also important as learning media, because they enable pupils to associate new knowledge with their own personal experience.

The issues of ownership and autonomy are important factors in the success of drama as a learning medium for these pupils. This is true of certain group activities also. Grant describes a lesson in which he and a group of fellow pupils are given the task of designing their own Roman Villa. For him the most important thing about this piece of work was the autonomy that he was allowed to exert:

> It was quite easy [...] We was allowed to make up our own thing. That was quite good, because we was allowed to make it all up ourselves. Didn't have to go to guidelines and that.

Having said this, Grant relates some of the information that he gathered from the teacher and used in his design:

> Well, Ms Bell said they was quite big [...], and they had quite a few rooms and that. So we knew. And they had quite a few pictures on the walls — can't remember what they was called — oh, [...] where you put little tiles on, sort of thing. [...] and she told us to do a bird's eye view.

Although Grant has used Ms Bell's information he is emphatic about pupil control and ownership:

> She didn't tell us what to do. I mean, we made up the number of rooms we wanted, and stuff like that. What shape we wanted it. And she told us there was usually a courtyard in the middle. [...] We sat in groups and worked out what we wanted to put in, but they weren't all identical.

The stress Grant places on the uniqueness of the final product highlights the importance of this aspect to him. We can see here how this sense of ownership relates to his own knowledge and understanding of the topic of study; what seems to be important is the fact that he has *used* this knowledge *for his own purposes*, in concert with other pupils.

The final theme of good social relationships between staff and pupils is also revealed to have powerful consequences for pupils' learning. It should be stressed that teachers' perceptions are closer to pupils' on this issue than the other two. There are, however, variations in the extent to which teachers see this social aspect as relating to learning; there is a tendency among the teachers in this study to see this quality as a 'setting' feature. For pupils, however, it is often the case that good quality social relations between teacher and class are seen to create particular kinds of learning opportunities. A graphic example of the effects of perceived differences in this respect is illustrated by Carmen, who describes the way in which opportunities to articulate her views and attitudes can be constrained and facilitated by different teachers. Carmen has recently arrived at her present school from a school elsewhere in the county:

> He's funny [Mr Fox], and my old teacher: nobody really liked her because [...] you couldn't do anything right. And with Mr Fox, he explains what you've done wrong. He doesn't shout at you. But this old teacher [did]. And also people could muck about in my old class, because they knew they'd get away with it [...]. [With] Mr Fox, you know not to mess him about, but he's fun as well.

The important educational consequence of this easy relationship is that:

> You can say whatever you want to Mr Fox [...]. [it] doesn't have to have [...] to be like what he thinks. [...] sometimes we were a bit frightened of that [former] teacher, and we didn't want to say what we thought.

Carmen then illustrates these claims with a description of written work that she has been doing in the previous lesson. The set task was to produce a piece of personal writing in the form of a diary, on the subject of an experience which is of personal importance. Carmen shows clearly the way in which such a task places the pupils in a potentially vulnerable situation, and how the relationship with the teacher has to be right before pupils will be prepared to take the risks necessary to approach it in a genuine and open way:

> [what I wrote] was the sort of thing you wouldn't really have said in front of other teachers [...], because what we'd done was a bit weird in a way, and some people might not agree with it. Some people might think it's really stupid.

She goes on to describe an unusual and deeply personal experience.

Carmen's experience is echoed by many other pupils, who describe the ways in which the sense of security and acceptance, which they often perceive their teachers to possess, acts as a stimulus to their learning. Pupils attribute to this quality their willingness to articulate new and half formed ideas in class discussion, and so develop their thinking on a topic; it also enables them to ask questions, and initiate their own and others' learning activities. In short, the good quality of social relations in classrooms seems to create for pupils the opportunities, which we have seen they find to be so important, for engaging in purposeful interaction with subject matter and the appropriation of new knowledge. Without this quality pupils believe that their need to be actively involved in their learning would be thwarted.

Conclusion

Evidence presented here suggests that there is substantial commonality between teacher and pupil perspectives on what effective learning is and what teachers do to facilitate it. When we come to look in detail, however, at the ways in which teachers and pupils talk about the relationship between teaching and learning we find some important differences in their perceptions. Pupils exhibit a clearer and more detailed understanding than their teachers of how particular teaching strategies interact with their learning processes. Related to this are differences in the range of considerations employed by teachers and pupils in their estimate of the appropriateness and effectiveness of learning experiences. Whilst pupils tend to focus on the links between learning experiences and learning processes, teachers employ a wider range of considerations, some of which occasionally lead teachers to adopt strategies and methods which are not conducive to effective learning.

The apparent conflict which is thus identified might well be attributed to tensions that are often perceived to be inherent in the teacher role: for example, tension between the obligations to facilitate learning and maintain order in the classroom, or between the aim of developing pupils' subject skills, and the aim of 'covering' a prescribed programme of study. It would seem that whilst teachers are aware of such tensions, their preferred solutions sometimes result in the implementation of teaching strategies that are detrimental to pupil learning. Such outcomes are clearly unintended and undesired by teachers, and are based, in part at least, on teachers' lack of detailed knowledge about precisely how children learn. It is suggested, therefore, that teachers would benefit from a greater knowledge of the kinds of processes and strategies that pupils employ in order to promote their own learning, if they were to use such knowledge in their responses to the tensions they experience.

This study shows that pupils can be a rich source of information about the relationship between teaching and learning. Given the availability of this source, it seems only logical to suggest that teachers should employ consultation with pupils on these issues in the pedagogical planning and evaluation processes. This study would also suggest that the fruits of such consultation would be of value to curriculum planners, enabling them to avoid measures which at present appear to undermine teacher effectiveness.

References

Brown, S. and McIntyre, D. (1993) *Making Sense of Teaching*. Milton Keynes: Open University Press.

Desforges, C. and McNamara, D. (1977) One man's heuristic is another man's blindfold: Some comments on applying social science to educational practice. *British Journal of Teacher Education* 3 (1), 27–39.

— (1979) Theory and practice: Methodological procedures for the objectification of craft knowledge. *Journal of Teacher Education* 28 (6), 51–5.

Powney, J. and Watts, M. (1987) *Interviewing in Educational Research*. London: Routledge.